# Praise for "Raw Coping Power"

*Dr. Bennett is an undisputed leader in the field of organizational wellness and particularly stress management. Having worked with him and observed his commitment to moving research into practice, I am excited about the excellent literary work he has produced.* **Raw Coping Power** *is more gentle than its title suggests; but just as serious. Using true stories for insight and impact, Dr. Bennett directs the reader to look within to his own path and then lights the way to make the journey easier. I felt that my friend was with me and I believe he was. He will be there for you, too. This is a powerful inspirational resource that will build strength and resilience for anyone. I hope you enjoy it as much as I did.*

Connie Tyne, Vice President of External Affairs
The Cooper Institute

*Resilience is among our most essential attributes, but it is routinely subject not only to wear and tear, but neglect. With obvious expertise, clear compassion, keen insight, and genuine wisdom, Joel Bennett explains why, and how, to cultivate this inner source of strength - and live a better life as a result.*

David L. Katz, MD, MPH, FACPM, FACP
Director, Yale University Prevention Research Center

**Raw Coping Power** *skillfully provides the principles and lenses you need to help you to tap into life differently. Having coached and counseled individuals and groups about body-mind-spirit, I've heard amazing stories about inner strength and getting back to just being. What I really like about* **Raw Coping Power** *is the tool box that nudges you along this path of self-exploration and life fulfillment. As a 4th stage prostate cancer survivor, I wake every morning recognizing I've been given another day to move beyond the "C" word and choose to thrive, experience and share my joy. Be open to the journey, be open to just being. Let* **Raw Coping Power** *unleash the raw, life energizing, spirit deep within you.*

William B. Baun, EPD, CWP, FAWHP
Wellness Officer, MD Anderson Cancer Center
President, National Wellness Institute

*Dr Joel Bennett is a bona fide thought leader, his work spot on, timely, and powerfully practical.* **Raw Coping Power** *is an accessible "system", helping individuals, teams, and workplaces to tap their inherent capacity to transform stress into a positive learning force. This book both inspires AND shows the way! With decades on the front lines of the wellness and integrative medicine revolutions, I enthusiastically declare this program "required" for executives, department heads and consultants. The system, formatting, stories, examples, and exercises make the concepts and ideas accessible and implementable. Excellent contribution, Dr. Bennett!*

Dr. Roger Jahnke, OMD
Author, "The Healer Within" and Director and Chief Instructor of the Institute of Integral Qigong and Tai Chi

*We all complain about stress, but with Dr. Joel Bennett's new book* **Raw Coping Power** *you can now re-envision those complaints as positive stepping stones to a life of thriving and flourishing. This book is a handy guide for revealing the hidden teaching power of stress. By blending real-world stories with research, Dr. Bennett makes a compelling case that each of us has a mostly untapped power to thrive, and the exercises actually take you there! A must read for anyone, especially those who wish to reveal new potential within their daily lives.*

Michaela Conley, MA, MCHES, CSMS
Founder and President: Health Promotion Live, HP Career.Net

**Raw Coping Power: From Stress to Thriving** *is condensed wisdom wrapped in a high impact took kit. Rather than kill us, successful stress skills enable us to life well – to thrive! The sympathetic arousal of the stress response is essential to survival while activating the parasympathetic system enables us to positively thrive. We need both, as Dr. Joel Bennett knows. His 7 basic principles and 10 different lenses are well anchored in this core psychophysiology and leading edge science as well as practice. The 31 tools available enable the user to select the best fit for their individual and collective wellbeing.*

James Campbell (Jim) Quick
Professor of Leadership & Organizational Behavior
John and Judy Goolsby – Jacqualyn A. Fouse Endowed Chair
The University of Texas at Arlington

*Raw Coping Power: From Stress To Thriving takes on stress in a refreshingly new way. Dr. Bennett presents us with a way of leveraging stress to our advantage by helping us see how we can reframe our experience of stress differently and respond in a way that helps us thrive. In this book "coping" does not mean toleration. Instead the author demonstrates how we can find the choices we really do have and act on them in self-enhancing ways. Stress is the vastly ignored area of wellness and yet is often the linchpin to health and well-being. Previous books on stress have usually looked at stress from a two-pronged approach of providing cognitive strategies for reducing our production of stress and providing physiological methods for minimizing our body's stress response. Joel Bennett takes things much further providing a way for individuals, organizations and helping professionals such as wellness coaches, therapists, counselors and healthcare providers to be of real value to those they serve.*

Michael Arloski, Ph.D., PCC, CWP
CEO and Founder Real Balance Global Wellness Services, Inc.
Dean of The Wellness Coach Training Institute

*Have you been looking for a source that provides a positive take on many of life's challenges, one that provides a framework for addressing these challenges, and tools that you can use and share with others? You need look no further. Joel Bennett has compiled a framework for looking at life's challenges that identifies principles for assessing the situation in his book Raw Coping Power. To complete this framework he provides a set of tools that you can use either by yourself or with others to build resilience and thrive.*

Professor Lois Tetrick, PhD
George Mason University

*Building one's ability to be resilient and "bounce back" in the face of adversity or challenge is foundational to improving one's sense of personal wellness or well-being. Raw Coping Power by Dr. Bennett is a virtual blue print and proven prescription for improving one's ability to cope with stress and enhance well-being. His real life examples and practical techniques will help anyone at any point on their path to well-being.*

David A. Sharar, Ph.D.
Managing Director, Chestnut Global Partners
Research Scientist, Chestnut Health Systems

*Fortunately, more and more employers recognize the importance of integrating an effective organizational and individual response to managing stress while building resilience. With **Raw Coping Power**, a very timely and evidence-based work, Dr. Bennett offers employers a valuable and proven resource for creating thriving organizations as well as thriving individuals.*

Kathy Greco, LMSW

Vice President (leading EAP industry specialty company)

*This book offers a useful guide to the discovery of your inner strength. We all need guidance to do better than we may realize was possible when we just follow the path of normal everyday life. Dr. Bennett has gathered a collection of insights that inspire, instruct and perhaps test the limits about what you think you can achieve. This book is an antidote to the demanding pace of our modern world, and offers a fresh perspective that is both optimistic and realistic about all the little things at work, at home, and in our heads that can keep us stuck in a rut and feeling hopeless at times. Taking care of yourself allows you more energy to share with loved ones, work colleagues and your community. The principles, perspectives and tools described in **Raw Coping Power** are based on the experience of someone who has spent his career studying and assisting leaders and organizations in how to be healthier - how to thrive in spite of the problems and limits that seem to be in place. Joel is well-respected as a scientist and trainer and has earned the right to focus his considerable intellect on this topic. Now you can benefit from his wisdom and wit. Reading this book can radically change you for the better. At the very least, following these practices may allow you to see yourself in a different, more positive, and more stress-free light.*

Mark Attridge, PhD, MA

President, Attridge Consulting; Workplace Health Researcher

# Raw Coping Power

## From Stress to Thriving

Joel B. Bennett, PhD

Organizational Wellness

Fort Worth, Texas

Joel B. Bennett | Organizational Wellness
3221 Collinsworth St. (Suite 220)
Fort Worth, Texas, 76109 - USA
www.organizationalwellness.com | www.rawcopingpower.com

NOTE TO READERS: This publication contains the opinions of its author.
Information and techniques presented are for preventive purposes and
should not be considered as a substitute for medical or professional advice.
The book is sold with the understanding that the author and publisher are
not providing licensed professional services. For such services, the reader
should consult with a medical, health, or other professional. The author and
the publisher specifically disclaim all responsibility for any liability, loss or
risk, personal or otherwise, which is incurred as a consequence, directly or
indirectly, of the use and application of any of the contents of this book. The
author did not interview any of those individuals or celebrities featured in
this book. Descriptions provided are from information publicly available.

Bennett, Joel B.
        Raw coping power : from stress to thriving / Joel B. Bennett, PhD.
        pages cm
        Includes bibliographical references.
        LCCN 2014904519
        ISBN 978-0-9915102-0-7 (pbk.)
        ISBN 978-0-9915102-1-4 (e-book)
        1. Stress management.        I. Title.
        RA785.B46 2014                155.9'042
                        QBI14-600046

# CONTENTS

# KEY LISTS

To all who find the inspiration
to make the best of a difficult situation
and then patiently go about changing the world.

*Some people grumble that roses have thorns;*

*I am grateful that thorns have roses.*

Alphonse Karr

# Foreword

PERSONAL AND JOB-RELATED STRESS—as source points for many problems—are perhaps the most overlooked areas in public health, in the workplace, and even among providers of health promotion and wellness programs. Research clearly shows that stress is a direct cause of a large proportion of diseases and decreased productivity, yet we spend most of our health care dollars on addressing the symptoms of stress rather than the stress itself. This blind spot is most egregious in the area of workplace wellness.

There is currently an overemphasis on health risk assessments and coaching and campaigns for diet, exercise, and specific topics such as hypertension, diabetes, tobacco use, and other commonly occurring risk factors and chronic diseases. All this is important work, but if employees work in an unhealthy and continually stressed work environment, these efforts will have limited impact.

To be blunt, employers risk wasting their financial and human resources when they only focus on the short-term gains from wellness without addressing the long-term consequences of stress.

What is equally amazing is that there is an extensive and growing body of research showing that well-designed stress management programs work. The key term in that last sentence is "well-designed."

This means more than time-limited lunch-and-learn programs that educate employees on personal coping methods.

To be clear, it is very important to train workers in mind/body practices that help them reduce anxiety and depression and alleviate somatic symptoms—all of which get in the way of morale and productivity. At the same time, we know that these programs have optimal and more lasting effects when employers make efforts in the social environment at work, especially efforts that create compassionate leadership and positive teamwork, where workers encourage each other and have fun getting and staying healthy.

So we have a dual challenge. First, to get at the root of many health and productivity problems, we must address stress in the work set-ting and do so with clear intention and systematic efforts. Second, to do this most effectively, we must find ways to engage employers such that they start translating insights from science into practice—common practice, shared practice. This is not an easy challenge for many obvious reasons.

Perhaps the most important one is that employers—as a reflection of society in general—either are too busy to notice that stress is the problem, or if they do see it, they don't have the time or the tools to do anything different. Or even more common is the "chicken-egg" phenomenon whereby employers feel that they can't take the time to make these efforts because it will hurt productivity to do so. We are stuck in an outdated paradigm, in what Charles Tart called "a consensus trance." Given growing recognition of the costs of stress and disease, it may be time to wake up from this trance and start meeting the challenge.

We are now ready to take on that challenge. Just in the past few years a growing number of studies, popular books, and training pro-grams have been designed to enhance resilience. This is a promising sign. What is even more exciting—and is a core premise of this book—is that we can now look at stress in a whole new way, as Dr. Bennett is showing us: as a positive lever for bringing about transformation in our personal lives and in the work setting. Such an idea suggests that resilience may only be a stopping point along the way to even greater thriving and flourishing.

Clearly, the perspective, the principles, the lenses, and the tools he offers in *Raw Coping Power* are designed to facilitate such thriving and flourishing. They are designed to help us all meet the dual challenge described. The question is whether these ideas and tools will fall into the hands of those who can practice them and influence others to do so.

Actually I am very optimistic. It is a wonderful thing when we can take information and insights from science and deploy them for the greater good. My hope is that you will be part of that growing positive force.

Kenneth R. Pelletier, PhD, MD
Clinical Professor of Medicine
Clinical Professor of Family and Community Medicine
Professor of Public Health
University of Arizona School of Medicine
And University of California School of Medicine (UCSF)

# Preface

THE PURPOSE OF THIS BOOK IS TO help you wake up to what you already, at some level, know to be true about yourself and about life. That is, you have within you the ability to meet life head on, take the good with the bad, and actively make any type of stress your friend and your teacher.

I hope you will come to the realization not only that stress is part of life, but that you have some inkling there is more to it. That you can use difficulty and adversity to get your life back on track, keep your life moving in a positive direction, or actually transform your life into something much more wonderful than you have imagined. I want you to see this realization as a gift and greet difficulty with natural boldness and intelligence. You can do it! You have it in you.

The strength of the human spirit is perhaps the most cherished topic of all writers. I am talking not only about fiction but about the work of historians, biographers, business writers, self-help authors, and documentarians. They have as much to say as movie-makers, poets, novelists, playwrights, and the creators of comic-book super heroes.

If you are a parent, you probably know this striving at a deep level. You want this same resilience in your children, and you get anxious if you think they don't also have it within them. If you are an entrepreneur or business leader, you also know that you have to keep up with the many changes and trials of an ever-changing economy. At some point you realize that, as Marshall Goldsmith, the executive coach, says, "what got you here won't get you there" and so you reinvent yourself.

So there is obviously an abundance of cultural material available in every society, throughout history, and in our families and businesses attesting to the fact that we can survive challenge and adversity, and we can actually grow from and shine because of them. Further, we also love stories that dramatically describe people and groups as they overcome obstacles and achieve even higher levels of functioning and consciousness.

So why then does everyone complain about stress? Has the world become more stressful of late? It would seem just the opposite. The further back in time we go, the harsher were the stressors our ancestors faced. Is it possible that we only believe we experience more stress today, again at some deep level, because we need to have challenge, something to test our mettle, prove our resilience, and make us stronger? This is certainly something to consider.

But there is also the fact that we now live in a more time-compressed world. On one hand, our rapidly emerging technologies make life less harsh for many while, on the other hand, these same technologies lead to a 24/7 barrage of information, with associated expectations, multi-tasking burdens, and potentials for conflict.

I would even venture to say that many of us have clamored for a front seat on the "stress bandwagon" or have gotten a wee bit drunk on the "stress Kool-Aid." We love our smartphone apps, various technical gadgets, the Internet, and other inventions that we adopt to lessen stress but that ultimately add to our strain.

This may be one of the greatest paradoxes of our modern world. Through the advances of science and technology we create external tools and aids that we believe will help us to save time and have more comfortable lives, but because of the ways we go about creating and using those tools, we actually experience less time and create sometimes highly demanding and compressed situations. We like to "do" so much with our stuff that we forget to just "be" with the simple pleasures. As John Lennon sang: "Life is what happens to you while you are busy making other plans."

I believe that one solution to this paradox is to turn our attention away from "doing" things with these "external" tools and return to a state of "being" in which we cultivate or tap into those "internal" tools that give us greater strength, happiness, and integrity. And that is the purpose of this book. But this changing direction—from the exterior to the interior—is quite difficult for many reasons. Chief among them is that our society does not currently value such "being."

You probably know what I mean if you use a computer, smartphone, or an electronic tablet for your occupation or if you spend any personal time surfing the Internet, downloading apps or music, or chatting on Facebook. But you may *really* experience what I mean if you feel compelled to stay current on these ever-evolving miracles of communication or if you suspect that you may be spending so much time with them that you neglect key parts of your life.

But these pressures (job-related or self-imposed) are just one reason why turning inward is difficult. There is another reason, and one that I think is a thousand times more important. It has to do with the fact that you have likely fallen asleep. One way of knowing whether you have fallen asleep is if you spend an inordinate amount of time in external activities: watching movies or reading stories about how *others* have been strong and resilient. That is right. The first sentence of this preface made it clear that the answer is inside you, not outside.

I want you to wake up to something and start using that precious and powerful inner resource to change your life. The cultural aides—movies, stories, games, videos, self-help guides—are helpful to the degree that they spur you on. But you also need the knowledge, the vision, and the tools to put that inspiration into effect. The question to ask yourself is not whether you are asleep but how do you awaken.

Just asking this question will be the first step. If you make the effort, you will be led to some self-knowledge. The principles in the first chapter of this book are intended to help you wake up to your own inner knowledge and to step off the "stress bandwagon" that everybody is on.

But you have to go past just self-awareness. You also have to start seeing. A new pair of glasses may help. Actually, a new set of lenses. These are provided in the second chapter of the book. And I am not making this stuff up. The research is showing us a new way of seeing the world that points clearly to this inner capacity to transform crippling stress into healthy resilience. Three cheers for science!

Now what I am about to say may lead some readers to question whether they should purchase this book or have regrets about doing so. First, I believe that if you really know—that is, you can deep down know that stress will *always* be your friend and teacher—then you may not even need the principles to guide you. Second, if you currently see *all* stressors as guiding your (stress-to-thriving) transformation, then you may not even need the lenses I share. The goal of both inner *knowing* and deep *seeing* is to abide in the place of strong *being* inside yourself.

This raw coping power is much more a state of being than it is a state of doing. The goal is *being* rather than *doing*, and the new lenses will hopefully be your corrective lenses to lessen the stress associated with always doing, doing, doing and enhance the health benefits associated with being.

Third, if you have knowledge and corrective lenses, then you don't really need the tools also provided in this book. As I said before, the "real" tools we need are already within us. We have just fallen asleep and have forgotten they are there. The best among all types of counselors—psychologists, wellness coaches, therapists—really help us get back in touch with our own inner resources anyway.

So, to repeat. You do not need this book if you are already awake. You know your own raw coping power, you have the vision to see how to use it, and you practice it regularly. By regularly, I mean every day.

But I am betting—and I did take the time to write this—that you might need at least a little help in one of these areas. I am betting that you could use a reminder or two, some tips, or just a good solid nudge. Maybe something to get your life back on a solid and even keel. Interestingly, it is the keel of a boat, or the origin of the phrase "even keel," that will provide our first story in *Raw Coping Power*.

The keel of a boat is the center spine or structural beam around which the entire hull of the ship is built. It is often the very first thing that is built and laid into place to form the "cradle" of a ship. There is an important ceremony when shipbuilders lay the keel as it represents the real structural birth of the ship. Historians believe that much of the expansion of early civilization and of world exploration depended upon the creation of the keel in early ship building following the Egyptian empire. In other words, without the sturdiness and structure that a keel provided, other smaller boats such as canoes and rafts lacked the resilience to weather long voyages of exploration, commerce, and the expansion of a country's domain.

The phrase or idiom "even keel" is reported as meaning a "state of normality; when the ship's keel is perfectly horizontal and her fore and aft draught are the same" (from Merriam-Webster) or "in a state of balance; steady; steadily" (from Dictionary.com). In common usage, we use sentences such as this: "If Jane can keep on an even keel and not panic, she will be all right" or "Try to keep on an even keel and not get upset so easily."

The truth is that, in real ship maneuvering and sailor jargon, a ship that floats on a perfectly even keel will be almost impossible to steer (for example, Aircraft Carriers). It is customary to be a bit "off-center" to keep good momentum and steering capacity. Yes, not only is the phrase "even keel" inaccurate, it is not really the ideal situation.

Why do I take the time to talk so much about keels? First, remember that, at one time, a keel on a boat provided the structure that led to a revolution in world exploration. Second, it would seem that to keep moving forward in life, we have to always be a little off-course—not too much but just enough to stay on top of things. These two features about keels can serve as an image for your own raw coping power.

We each have our own keel, our raw coping power. I could say, "Wake up and find your keel" or "You have a lot more strength than you know." And, as we move through life, we are always off-course, sometimes only slightly and sometimes in wide, even crazy, arcs. I could say, "Pay attention" or "Don't worry about staying on an even keel too much and instead see what you can learn from these disruptions" or just "Keep steering!"

And so this book is written to help you do all of these. I appeal to different sensibilities in hopes that some messages might work better than others. Some readers will learn most from the principles, while others will enjoy the lenses more. Still others will gravitate to using one or more tools. In a way, I am inviting you to build a new ship for your life—a whole new way of looking at stress. And in a way, I hope this book helps you find your keel for that new ship.

# Introduction:
# Images of Adversity,
# Stories of Resilience

THROUGHOUT HISTORY, PEOPLE HAVE exhibited raw coping power—the subject of this book. Do you recognize any of these people?

A YOUNG MAN IS BETRAYED by his brothers and sold into slavery. Through fortune and use of talent the young man is able to not only make the most of his situation but gain the recognition of authorities. He is appointed to a powerful political position. Later, through his new identity unbeknown to his brothers, the young man shows them forgiveness and shares the benefits of his new power.

A YOUNG WOMAN, AFTER BEING KIDNAPPED by natives who nearly destroyed her home, is taken almost 800 miles away. She manages to escape and travel by foot, mostly through the winter months, and finds her way back to her husband after forty days of living off roots and berries. She continues her new life, contributing to her community in her remaining years.

A MUSICAL COMPOSER CONTINUES TO WRITE and perform music after suffering hearing loss and debilitating bouts of depression and illness. His latter compositions grow in beauty and depth and become among the most widely performed pieces for generations and throughout the world.

A YOUNG WOMAN, DYING OF A TERMINAL DISEASE, inspires her sister to take action to invest in research and give others hope in the face of their own struggles with the disease. As a result, an organization is formed that raises billions of dollars for groundbreaking research, community health outreach, advocacy, and programs in more than fifty countries. The efforts of this single organization result in improved survival rates from the disease.

For those of you playing along here with the home game, the forgiving young man is Joseph from the Old Testament; the young woman who was kidnapped was Mary Draper Ingeles (1732–1815) who escaped from Apache abductors in 1755; the musical composer is, of course, Beethoven; and Nancy Brinker founded the world's premier breast cancer foundation in memory of her sister, Susan G. Komen.

The history of humanity, in all of its intricate details and in all of our highly personal journeys, reveals a tale of collective human resilience, as these stories show. And by resilience, I mean more than mere survival but an ability to learn from such survival and apply that learning to growth—even radical growth.

This great human tale has been told through the stories of nations, races, families, and organizations as well as individuals. It is also reflected to us in the mirrors of our myths and legends, especially through the stories of religions, heroes, and great leaders. Yet, at the most intimate level, resilience informs each of our own personal stories. Each of us has within us the capacity to grow from, and thrive despite, all types of adversity.

This story is happening around us all the time—most likely in the lives of those we interact with every day at work, in our common shopping or travel routines, and among our friends and family. You may even have your own personal favorite—a book you read, a movie or show you saw—that inspires because it helps you tap your unique personal capacity, building strength and hope. The following real-life examples may help you recall such a story.

Here are a few more captivating tales in our random walk through history. They show how diverse and thoroughly woven and connected lie the strands of resilience in our collective consciousness.

My goal in sharing these capsule accounts is to help you remember your own inner resources. Many of these are popular and may be recognizable, while others are less known. Each is stripped down to its barest nature without identifying the person or source.

Bring your attention not to one specific example but to a common phenomenon and, more importantly, to the realization that resilience has been available to all of humanity, despite race, gender, historical era, geography, or nation. Raw coping power is not simply an individual resource. Its finest expression might be found in small and large groups, in families, communities, organizations, and in humanity as a whole.

A GENERATION OF PEOPLE FROM A single ethnic group was forced to leave their homes and livelihoods by governmental authorities. As a result, almost one third of the 12,000 exiles were killed through disease or drowning. After many trials, many families settled in a new land thousands of miles away and are now a thriving community contributing great vibrancy and culture to the society around them.

A WOMAN'S BELIEF IN NONVIOLENCE and democracy led her to continue, over several decades, to protest military rule in her country. Much of this time she was placed under strict military surveillance and not allowed to travel. Her perseverance in expressing her views inspired millions of people and led to international awards and recognition.

A FILMMAKER DECIDES TO TELL THE STORY of a humanitarian hero who saves the lives of persecuted refugees who would likely have been killed without his intervention. Because of popular and international response to the film, a foundation is established that helps to successfully archive 52,000 testimonies and 105,000 hours of video, which are fully cataloged and translated into thirty-two languages. This project informs classrooms around the world, educating children about the dangers of prejudice.

A MAN ATTEMPTS TO COMMIT SUICIDE after his wife divorces him and his beloved pet dies. His children find him before he dies, and he begins a journey of recovery. This man, a celebrity, openly shares his struggle and hardship and has role-modeled the importance of staying connected to people as part of resilience. He claims. "There is a saying, 'What doesn't kill you makes you stronger.' That became real for me. It made me closer to people."

A BEST-SELLING AUTHOR CONTINUES to write popular books—using a scribe to pen his ideas—after developing a debilitating disease that prevents him from clearly expressing his ideas in writing. His publisher and the public did not even know about the disease, yet his new books continue to receive praise and achieve record sales.

THROUGH HER YEARS AS A TEENAGER and young adult, a woman overcomes poverty, exposure to violence, mistreatment due to her race, and teachers who question her abilities. By learning through these challenges she creates a foundation that goes on to serve nearly 100,000 teens. She becomes a best-selling author and is highly sought after as a motivational speaker.

A MAN WHO SUFFERS FROM SERIOUS ADDICTION is supported by others in his workplace to help him find a way to recovery. As a result of his coworkers' compassion and support, he is gainfully employed and now inspires others in his work community.

Stories such as these, known and told in every period of history, remind us that there is an innate capacity within human beings—both individually and collectively—not only to cope with the most horrific of problems but also to use these tragedies as a source for renewal and progress.

The capsules here are true and should, by themselves, serve as encouragement. Many of us also turn to historical or pure fiction to gain inspiration from those characters who survived challenge and went on to fight for good outcomes, social justice, or some other transcendent value.

Some of the Acadian people, the first story, who were expelled from Canada later settled in Louisiana and are now known as Cajuns. Their plight is similar to that of the Cherokee along the Trail of Tears and is emblematic of the resilience not only of an entire culture of Native Americans but of many groups that have migrated to the United States or to any other country from their native lands of oppression.

The woman under house arrest is Aung San Suu Kyi, the opposition leader in her home country of Myanmar. She has since been freed. The filmmaker Steven Spielberg honored the work of Oskar Schindler in the movie *Schindler's List* (1993). The man who is saved from suicide is Cesar Millan, widely known for his television series *Dog Whisperer*. The best-selling author is Martin Cruz Smith, author of *Gorky Park* (1981), who found ways to overcome his Parkinson's disease with the help of his wife as scribe. The motivational speaker who has helped many teenagers is Lisa Nichols, author of *No Matter What* (2011).

The man recovering from addiction is actually someone I know through a colleague. He represents thousands of other workers in recovery, many of whom I have been privileged to meet through delivering *Raw Coping Power* training to workplaces and in military settings. Their stories of recovery are echoed by those who have grown up with an alcoholic parent, adult children of divorce, and those with diverse types of physical and mental disability.

These examples are stories of superheroes, and the world's cultures are full of superheroes of all types (real and otherwise), ranging from the farm girl Dorothy who confronts the Wizard of Oz to the red demon Hellboy who fights against paranormal villains. Many individuals play video or other types of games that allow them to take on the role of hero, ranging from a Pokémon trainer who seeks to expand her or his collection of species to a first-person killer in Call of Duty electronic games. Some may not consider such games to portray stories of heroes believing they convey little meaning or depth in plot line. However, multi-player gamers often project their own images and fantasies that give a personal sense of mastery or strength. Achieving or winning in such games strengthens their inner sense of resilience.

## WHAT STORIES RESONATE WITH YOU?

Each one of us has our own unique preference or liking for stories where challenges are overcome and transformed for positive outcomes. In particular, we may be drawn to a certain type of character or hero. The term *archetype* is often defined as the original pattern or model from which all things of the same type have come. The psychologist Carl Jung hypothesized that these archetypes reside like a template in the historical and collective unconscious of humanity. These archetypes can vary in great detail within any given culture or work of art.[1]

Let's say that you like stories, books, or movies about romance and lovers who overcome obstacles to find each other. The archetype of *Lover*—which is actually inside you—is resonating with romantic stories and looking to express itself, learn, and grow from the experience of reading or watching the movie. Other common archetypes include the Child, the Orphan, the Magician, Explorer, Warrior, Martyr, King or Queen, Detective, Healer, and Sage, as just some examples. Importantly, each of these archetypes expresses raw coping power in different ways. The Orphan learns to make it in the world without parental support. The Detective must persist in looking for evidence and solving the problem in the face of danger.

The popularity of different movie genres in a given period may reveal how a segment of society views raw coping power. For example, in the past few years there has been considerable growth in movies and television shows on the subject of vampires. The archetype of *Vampire* is rich with meaning and includes hunger for love, powerful intimacy and eroticism, dependency, and the ability to live in two worlds and cheat death, an ultimate form of resilience.

But the point does not have to do with my interpretation or the interpretation of anyone besides yourself. Each of us can learn about our own raw coping power by exploring why we personally like certain stories and characters. A basic grasp of archetypes may help you re-cast these heroes as golden keys to the door of your inner power.

True stories, the recognition or the need for heroes, works of fiction, and role-playing video games provide examples of our innate drive for resilience. We resonate with these reflections because they trigger some familiar yet often vague image in our brains, something not always conscious but that feels like a basic life force, a propensity to strive and actualize our destiny. This idea is not new. Many different concepts proposed by psychologists speak to this in-born motivation, our instinctual desire to be effective in realizing our capacities.[2]

You may have heard of some of these concepts and their proponents, such as Maslow's theories on self-actualization, Holocaust survivor psychologist Frankl and his work on the will to find meaning, White's effectance motive, Deci and Ryan's published articles on self-determination, the concept of Flow as outlined by Csikszentmihalyi, and Bandura's theories on self-efficacy, Maddi on hardiness, and Manz on self-leadership.

Taken together, these concepts, most of them subject to scientific investigation, bring a new and valuable contribution to our understanding of resilience and of our ability to thrive under stress. The hundreds of studies that have been conducted on stress and resilience further attest to the fact that human beings have this wonderful capacity that I have called raw coping power.

In addition, many popular self-help books have been written to guide individuals in their quest to strengthen this capacity. Given all this background and attention, what is different or unique about the concepts in *Raw Coping Power?*

When the stories, theories, and research are combined, they all point to an emerging set of principles, lenses, and tools that can now be used to help us further develop our raw coping power. More accurately, they better allow us to recall this capacity in the different challenges we face as individuals, as groups, and as society.

We now know enough about stress that we can use our history, our many stories of resilience, and insights from our research. We can bring all this together in a new way not only to help people respond to stress but to prevent many stress-related problems from ever happening. *Raw Coping Power* is really a prevention program that offers a new and practical synthesis of our accumulated and interdisciplinary knowledge about resilience and thriving.

By practical, I hope that you will treat *Raw Coping Power* as a manual, a "how to" or DIY (do it yourself) guidebook. Despite the abundant research and autobiographical insights we have at our disposal, many still suffer because they lack a method for grasping this knowledge. This may be due to the fact that a simple yet systematic approach is needed, one that is informed by an integration of new ideas, together with research and experience.

The first chapter, *The 7 Basic Principles*, presents seven basic ideas informed by past research and my experience delivering dozens of stress management programs to different types of organizations. These basic principles provide a firm foundation for any program in stress management. They speak to a proactive skill that can be learned rather than a reactive tendency to succumb.

Almost every day we are presented with the choice to either learn or to be lazy in the face of challenge. This challenge can be a simple stressor such as being cut off in traffic, having to wait in a long line at the grocery store, or having a technical problem with your phone or computer. The challenge can be more complicated such as an interpersonal conflict at work, a family hardship due to illness, or an unforeseen financial loss.

Whether the challenge is simple or complex, our brains are wired to make a choice as to whether to learn greatly from the situation or to ignore it or to merely do our best to cope with it. The 7 Basic Principles chapter guides us to move forward in the direction of learning and radical growth.

The chapter on *The 10 Different Lenses* reviews ten diverse contemporary models or ways of seeing stress and resilience. Some of these lenses come from my company's award-winning programs Team Awareness and Team Resilience, but most are taken from recent studies that suggest we can now see stress in its more positive light. Spoiler alert: Not all stress is bad!

I should acknowledge here the groundbreaking works and "lenses" provided by the endocrinologist Hans Selye (1907–1982) for his concept of eustress and the medical sociologist Aaron Antonovsky (1923–1994) for his concept of salutogenesis.[3]

No need to stress over these terms. Let me explain.

*Eustress* may be defined as positive stress that leads to viewing stressors as challenges and subsequently to positive coping, adaptation, growth, and community. It differs from *distress*, which leads to viewing stress as a hindrance and unhealthy physiological responses.

Eustress gives us a feeling of fulfillment and other positive emotions, and we even participate in activities (such as athletic challenges) for the purpose of eustress.

*Salutogenesis* refers to the capacity for some individuals to continue to have health despite their exposure to significant hardships that might cause others to succumb and fall ill. Antonovsky coined the term for two reasons. First, to distinguish it from pathogenesis, which means the development of disease. Second, to counter the medical establishment's over-riding tendency to focus mainly on pathology or the causes of illness (pathogenesis) rather than to build health.

The final chapter, *The 31 Tools for Thriving*, gives instruction on thirty-one various exercises, many of which can be completed in ten to fifteen minutes. These tools put the principles of raw coping power into practice so that you can begin to see the world through the new set of lenses.

You may go directly to the Tools section and do the work there. Note that doing any one exercise just once may not be sufficient and that you might gain the most benefit by repeated practice, especially if you do the practice with others in a safe group setting.

Alternately, the tools may be most beneficial after fully understanding the principles and the lenses. They are not designed to be practiced for their own sake but with the goal in mind of creating eustress and salutogenesis for yourself as well as for others.

Many of the elements in *Raw Coping Power* are derived from my consultation in training that seeks to promote a healthy work culture where workers can experience collegiality in a transformative way. I, and those whom I have trained as facilitators, have worked with more than a hundred companies or agencies training close to 30,000 employees through the years, both in the United States and abroad.[4]

So this is not as much a "self"-help book as it is a "social"-help book. The importance of compassion, social connection, and support underlies nearly all of the stories of resilience noted earlier. Rarely is any real hero a lone hero. I believe the real heroes are those groups, teams, and workplaces that value the importance of a healthy culture where everyone learns and thrives together.

Because many of my insights about stress come from the workplace, I want readers to see the relevance of this book for work. Here, you will find the lenses of *Team Awareness* and *Manager Potentiation* and the tools of *Work-Life Borders* and *Job Crafting*. All aspects of this book can be used in work settings; these elements are just more work focused. An Appendix provides a few organizational-level tools that may be useful to human resources and their advisors.

Overall, my hope is that the principles, lenses, and tools are used in the service of creating social connections—at or away from work—for this is where they will have most success for you. And by nurturing these connections you stand to further humanity's story of resilience. You never know, your journey of resilience with friends, families, and colleagues might be the source of inspiration to some future generation.

YOUR INNER GUARDIAN[5]

EACH ONE OF US HAS A CENTRAL ASPECT of our being that witnesses events without being affected by those events. This aspect has been called different names in different spiritual and psychological traditions. There may be important differences among these names, but they do have in common the ability to stand apart from life events, see things freshly, and not "take effect."

You may call this inner guardian by any of these names: essence, witness, observer, pure self, higher self, superconciousness, the unadorned, diamond mind, beginner's mind, Bodhicitta (Buddhism), Satipatthāna (Buddhism), Shahid (Sufism), stillness within (Quakerism), Hesychia (Eastern Orthodox Church).

Many spiritual traditions suggest that extensive or routine practice is required to cultivate this inner witness. The idea that we have an inner guardian who not only protects us from stress but can also transform it is obviously not new. And readers should look to their own religious or spiritual preference to awaken this inner capacity.

In *Raw Coping Power*, the principles remind us that this guardian exists, the lenses are ways to look at the world through the vantage point of that guardian, and the tools are exercises to help awaken your knowledge that it is possible to see stress as your teacher and friend.

## HOW *RAW COPING POWER* CAN HELP YOU

This book can help you find ways to tap into your own resilience capacity—your raw coping power—on a regular basis. Just by knowing and embracing the principles, you can awaken that part of you, something I call an inner guardian, which knows how to use stress as a lever for self-betterment or as a bridge to become more calm, relaxed, and effective in your relationships and at work.

One woman I consulted with was able to calmly work through a break-up with her boyfriend because she knew that her values would eventually bring her a better life without him (see Principle #4). She is now happily married to a different man.

When you put on the different lenses, you will start to see how stress is somewhat over-rated as a negative force. Instead of complaining about life's irritants or succumbing to them, you will flip them around as golden opportunities. You move from stress to eustress and from pathogenesis to salutogenesis. In one example, our Team Resilience approach (see Lens #5) led coworkers to share their coping skills with one another such that their stress was reduced even in the midst of downsizing and store closings.

The different exercises in the tools chapter are equivalent to the various exercise and weight machines at the fitness club or gym. These tools help you develop your inner guardian. For example, physical fitness requires ongoing self-assessment and exercises for weight maintenance, fat loss, cardiovascular strength, muscle strength, muscle tone, and cardio endurance. In a parallel way, maintaining your raw coping power requires a regimen of activities for stress awareness, relaxation, problem solving, social support, focusing on the positive, and exploring your spiritual health.

The principles, lenses, and tools are designed to help in very specific and practical ways, as long as you practice them to the best of your ability. They all ask you to simply tap into your own raw coping power, just like the superheroes in the stories I have described in the introduction.

Let me explain how to do that. Actually, there are two parts to this explanation. First, suppose you have any of the following stressors. Just pick one or add your own current favorite:

- Job stress such as unreasonable timelines or workloads
- Family stress
- Job loss or fear of such loss
- Death of a friend or loved one including a beloved pet
- Pressure to join coworkers in unhealthy pursuits
- Disease
- A family member has an addiction problem
- Your teenager runs off with a motorcycle gang
- Aging parent becomes your responsibility
- A loud sound from your neighbor keeps you awake
- You have a harsh argument with your spouse
- Your car breaks down
- Your micro-managing boss picks on you for no apparent reason

Depending on how you observe, witness, and frame these life events and how you respond, any of these can lead to problems with your energy, health, ability to concentrate or relate with others, and work performance. You might argue that car problems pale in comparison to dealing with the death of a family member. The fact is that each of us, depending on our life circumstance, can have strong emotional reactions to different life events, no matter how big or small.

Second, notice that in the previous paragraph I said "depending on how you observe, witness, and frame" and also "depending on our life circumstance." The idea that we have an internal observer or witness that stands apart from life and can help us through challenges is central to most spiritual paths. It is also key to stress management. This book will help you tap into and cultivate the strength of your own inner observer. Again, we call this an inner guardian.

The research is also very clear that context matters: how we frame and respond to events as well as the situations surrounding events are as important as the events themselves.[6] Not all stressors of the same type need to have a similar effect on us. Cesar Millan quoted Friedrich Nietzsche when he said: What doesn't kill us can make us stronger. We have the ability to rewrite negative life events and see them as core gifts that shape us into better human beings.

By using the ideas and tools in this book you will learn to reframe negative events, choose more skillful responses, and improve your overall sense of effectiveness. To give you a sense that these techniques work, let's take a second look at some of the previous stressors, this time with real examples.

*Job stress.* In one of our studies using tools similar to those here, we found that workers learned to choose more positive ways to unwind after work, such as exercise, spending time with friends, meditating, or praying.[7] Many of them had hard jobs but instead of complaining, they now focused on healthier ways to unwind from those jobs. See Tools #16 and #17.

*Family stress.* In our work with the military, pre-deploying service members became more knowledgeable about and willing to use resources for their families.[8] Knowing that their families had resources resulted in stress reductions. Many of these soldiers were at risk for post-traumatic stress disorder (PTSD) not only because of exposure to war but because of family concerns and the perceived inability to do anything to help. See Tool #12.

*Job loss.* One manager was concerned about job loss and career derailment if she took time from work to attend to personal issues. The training we provided reduced her stigma for seeking help, and she was able to get consultation to solve her dilemma and to keep her job at the same time. Tool #19 on problem solving is similar to the process this manager used.

*Peer pressure.* In several studies with Team Awareness (Lens #8), the entire climate surrounding unhealthy use of alcohol improved.

Overall, employees felt less pressure to join colleagues in drinking. As a result, the entire climate of the work setting also improved.

*Aging parent.* One worker was very stressed about having to deal with his mother, who was starting to show signs of dementia. Through use of several communication and peer-to-peer tools, he found another colleague with a similar problem and together they were able to help each other. These workers used Tool #30 on Really Listening.

*Your boss.* Managers have their own special set of stressors that can lead them to be less than fun to work with. One of our programs, training managers in a more compassionate approach, led them to be less stressed and seen as better leaders by their associates.[9] See Lens #9 on Manager Pathways.

These are just a few examples. They each show that how we frame and respond to stress may not only alleviate the stress but actually lead to improvements in our life. And that is the whole idea behind *Raw Coping Power.* We can transform stress into a resource for resilience, for thriving, and for flourishing in life.

---

**Do You Provide Wellness or Stress Management Programs?**
If you would like to use some or all of the instruments in our tools chapter, please contact us for information on training and the training of trainers. We also provide copies of this book in quantity at attractive discounts. We also certify trainers in *Raw Coping Power, Team Awareness,* and *Team Resilience.*
Contact: learn@organizationalwellness.com and (817) 921-4260.

# | 1 |

# The 7 Basic Principles

HERE THEY ARE, THE BASIC PRINCIPLES of raw coping power. They don't mean much to you right now, but this chapter explores each one in detail.

> 1 ▪ We are designed to learn so much so that we deliberately place ourselves in stressful situations for the purpose of growth and transformation.
>
> 2 ▪ We can systematically transform our approach to stress from "the kiss of death" to "the spice of life."
>
> 3 ▪ We each have an innate or in-born raw coping power; we can tap into this and work with stress as part of our own transformation.
>
> 4 ▪ Our values determine the level through which we process stress, from severe distress to a rich uplifting experience of thriving.
>
> 5 ▪ Social groups can help others tap into their raw coping power and together transform stress into an experience of thriving at the cultural level.
>
> 6 ▪ We can go beyond resilience and show audacity in our quest for conversion, peak experiences, flourishing, or thriving.
>
> 7 ▪ Our nervous system is a well-oiled feedback system that allows us to deal with stress at every stage.

Our nervous system is so wonderfully designed to learn that we deliberately place ourselves in stressful situations for the purpose of learning, growth, and transformation.

WHEN WE PAY CAREFUL ATTENTION to our mind and body, we see that stress is not a single, uniform thing or event. We perceive something internal (mind) and external (environment) followed by an immediate or short-term response, a decision as to how to respond, an experience of tension, and quite often we learn something as a result. We adapt to the situation. Paying mindful attention to these factors, we have less chance of accumulated tension, memories, regrets, worries, or concerns. What we label as stress often refers more to these accumulations than to stress itself.

For example, Bob is a manager who continually dealt with a colleague, Gary, whom he felt was not doing the expected level of performance. Bob got anxious whenever he had to interact with Gary. He even woke up with neck and back tension on days when he knew they were to work together in meetings. The anxiety and tension built up to the point that Bob decided it was time to do something.

In his case, he first realized that he was worrying too much about something he could not directly control. This brought his tension down. Next, being more relaxed, he was able to discern when Gary was actually doing specific things that he felt he had the right to comment on. Having set his own stress aside, Bob was then able to communicate his needs in a calm way that Gary could hear.

Not only did Bob's stress go away but the entire performance of the team improved. As a result, Bob's skill as a manager was recognized by others. At first, all Bob thought about was how Gary caused him stress. But, as he slowed down, paid attention, and had positive adaptation, he learned new skills.

It helps to have an initial definition of stress. The one we will use for now is this:

Stress: An experience of *responding* to harm or potential harm or *stressors* that can tax your ability to cope, producing tension or *strain* and/or lead to productive learning or *adaptation*.

This definition will evolve as we cultivate specific skills and competencies that transform stress from a cause of problems to an opportunity for growth.

Note four different components to this definition:

*Responding:* Stress does not solely exist "out there" or in our mental state. How we respond to stress shapes its impact on us.

*Stressors:* Life presents us with threats. Harmful or potentially harmful things exist both in the environment and, yes, also in our thoughts, feelings, and impulses.

*Strain:* Our brain and nervous system are masterfully designed to respond to harm in ways that produce tension. This signal says: "Take action to reduce the tension!" In its initial or natural state, strain is a means to the end of alleviation, not an end in itself. Ongoing strain is not natural when it is not followed by efforts to address it.

*Adaptation:* We can always learn from the previous factors of responding, stressors, and strains. Our nervous system helps us achieve productive learning so that we are able not only to deal with stress in the future but also to thrive.

When you consider that learning and adaptation are very often the goal or end state of most stress, it is easy to understand how we may deliberately place ourselves in stressful situations for the purpose of learning, growth, and transformation.

Contemplation of this four-part definition reveals stress is part and parcel of our evolution as human beings, at both the personal and species level. Our consciousness depends upon, and is a result of, how we negotiate our entry into, immersion in, and learning from stressful experiences. When seen in the right perspective, and when we have the skills to embrace it, stress brings a gift of awakening.

Let's return to the example with Bob. He awoke to the fact that he could pay better and more prompt attention to his strain and choose healthier responses. Looking back at this time in his career, Bob now considers Gary a real gift because it led Bob to learn in new ways.

This is just one example but the idea behind the principle is profound. You may say, "Bob didn't ask to work with Gary. Why would anyone go into a situation knowing that it would bring hardship, challenge, and stress?" My answer is that in some of our stressful situations we don't always get to choose (especially as children), while others we do participate in constructing. Nonetheless, it is how we respond that makes a world of difference.

I believe that most of us in most situations are aware at some level of what we are getting into. We may not be fully conscious of it. But the point of this first principle is just that. To help you to start to wake up. Look at the stress in your life with the idea that maybe you are in the situation to learn something, to find the gift. People are even able to reconstruct their past trauma in ways that help them to see, and celebrate, a hidden strength. This may not have been possible without the adversity. And, as a result of this new insight, their life is transformed.

We can systematically transform our entire approach to stress.
The obstacle we previously saw as a life of distress ("the kiss of
death") can become a bridge to a life of thriving ("the spice of life").

STRESS CAN BE THE SPICE OF LIFE or the kiss of death. It depends on how
we see it. There really is no stress, at least as we commonly think and
talk about it. Most of what we label "stress" is a creation of our own culture, due to lifestyle, or as a result of mental habits, a faulty labeling system, and a failure to make an effort to observe and remember.

Stress is a great teacher when we can see it for what it is, apply
proper labels to it, and use the right tools to address it.

We have learned to say, "I am under stress," or "Work stress is just
too much right now," or "I am having stress at home." Here, the term
*stress* often serves as a mask. We don't have to reveal to others—and
ourselves—what is really going on. In an unhelpful and self-fulfilling
way, the mask ends up being the real problem, rather than those
situations that we refer to as stressful. We can change our attitude
toward stress, take off the mask, and see things for what they are.
These three steps may take persistence and courage, but it is possible
to deal with even the most horrific of problems.

To be clear, our lives can include trauma. This includes witnessing
or experiencing violence, combat, war, disaster, sexual violation,
sudden death, disease, loss of bodily function, or loss of loved ones or
important social supports. There are also work habits and conditions

that produce such significant job strain or burnout that workers develop serious diseases. This includes an unhealthy work culture, workaholism, unsupportive managers and coworkers, heavy workloads, lack of control, repetitive work, lack of rewards for the effort put in, and exposure to environmental toxins and incidents, including customer mistreatment, sexual harassment, and abusive supervision.

Finally, certain family and relationship events and systems can produce mental distress including separation and divorce, abuse (verbal, emotional, and physical), family members with illness (mental and physical), long-term and unresolved conflict and grief, and caring for aging or dying relatives.

> How can you take the perspective that stress is either a teacher, a friend, a gift, or an opportunity?

So let's acknowledge that events such as trauma, job strain, burnout, dysfunction, and family problems cause stress. Real stress. It is important to label these accurately, apply specific tools to alleviate problems, and obtain professional support if needed.

But, for the most part, many of the occurrences we view as stress can be addressed through thoughtful application of simple techniques. Regular use of these tools—especially when done with others in a shared work or family environment—can promote recovery from traumatic exposure, job strain, burnout, dysfunction, and family problems. The key lies in applying a well-thought-out or systematic approach, using not just one tool but many different tools over time.

Studies on the most effective ways to reduce job-related stress suggest that it is important to focus on prevention and make improvements in the shared work environment.[1] These programs are systems-level approaches that primarily address the source of stressors such as job demands, poor communication, or long work hours. But these systems approaches also go further. They help train employees to better respond to stress, and, for those experiencing the symptoms of stress, they provide tools and resources to reduce or eliminate those symptoms.

Multi-pronged programs that help the overall work culture, or programs that gives more workers more tools, usually work much better than a single focus on teaching workers how to relax. In addition to providing *Raw Coping Power* training, it helps to do simple things such as making sure to have follow-up instead of one-shot work meetings, giving clear but anonymous opportunities to provide input, for example through the old-fashioned suggestion box, giving employees more opportunities for stress breaks, and providing other types of health promotion with team participation opportunities.

Like these studies have shown, we can transform our lives such that what we previously saw as a hindrance—the kiss of death—becomes a bridge to enlightenment—the spice of life. Results from the system-level studies include reductions in work stress, turnover, sickness absence, and suicide rates, and improvement in work climate, employee morale, job satisfaction, and communication.

## A NOTE ABOUT DEFINITIONS

Adaptation, resilience, and thriving are different from each other in important ways. When we are adapting, we are learning from a challenge. When we are resilient, we are demonstrating strength in the face of the challenge. When we thrive, we have either developed new strengths or tapped into hidden strengths. As a result, we become better, stronger, or smarter by having been in the challenging situation. When we thrive, we focus on the present moment and creatively move into a beneficial future. Our positive actions breed more positive actions. Our creative projects stimulate more positive projects. In contrast, resilience tends to focus more on bouncing back from the past. The goal of *Raw Coping Power* is to help you adapt and be resilient but, most of all, to thrive.

*We each have an innate raw coping power that allows us to transform stress into a source of thriving. We can work with stress as part of the terrain of our transformation.*

WE EACH HAVE THE INNATE ABILITY to deal with events considered as stressful. With such raw coping power, we can transform stress into opportunities for thriving. What might at first glance appear to us as stress can turn out to be a lever for a higher level of functioning. Indeed, the most difficult life challenges call us to tap into this innate capacity.

Raw coping power is a personal competency, but it is best to not rely on it alone to create the conditions that will foster optimal growth. We should cultivate healthy communication with others who also seek health, and supportive systems and environments.

For example, imagine working in a sedentary office job that provides little opportunity for growth and advancement. Your coworkers feel that their work is boring and routine too, and as a group you usually share homemade desserts and unhealthy snack food as a highlight of your work week.

Everyone is just going along to get along. Together, you have a choice of just tolerating the situation, griping, or doing nothing until you burn out or retire. Alternately, you can look for ways to be grateful for each other, support each other and start thinking of new and positive methods to make work meaningful. By openly communicating about your concerns, together you cultivate a solution-oriented attitude that by itself improves the social climate at work. This is not a make-believe situation. In addition to stress training, there are many easy-to-implement and effective activity programs available such as Booster Breaks, Instant Recess, or onsite stretching programs that require little to no cost.[2]

We can trust our raw coping power and seek out and work in supportive environments, and we can also take charge and create such environments within our current situations. As we do, we harness the power to live a fulfilling life, follow our dreams, contribute to society, and build a world where others can thrive and flourish.

Our willingness to meet difficulty is a direct way to tap into this raw coping power. When we are willing to expand our capacity for health, success, productivity, or abundance, we are more likely to greet stress as an opportunity rather than a hindrance.

Stress management is less about preparing for, and learning how to manage, difficulty and more about finding our inner passion, desire, and longing to grow and expand our capacity as human beings. We don't "deal" with stress. Instead, we work with it as part of the terrain of our transformation.

As with any terrain, we are served by a map and a compass—tools to plan and navigate. Our willingness to learn is a critical source of energy for the journey. It keeps us from succumbing to stress. Having like-minded travelers can also redirect us when we get lost or buoy us when we hit rough spots. But we also need tools for times when these resources are lacking.

The tools provided in the latter section of this book are designed to help you leverage stress for growth and transformation. It is best to see these supports as a healthy means to increase well-being. At the same time, it is important to avoid getting attached to any one method of support. Remember that tools are just the means to the end of tapping into your own natural healing power. Take what you need and leave the rest.

There are different levels through which we can process stressful experiences, from severe distress to a rich uplifting experience of thriving. Our values help determine what we settle for and our day-to-day willingness to raise our levels.

THE FIRST MAP OR TOOL TO ASSIST our transformation is our understanding of different levels of pain and happiness, our awareness and appreciation of our current level, and our tolerance for different levels. Each of us tends to have a "set-point."[3] That's the point we have been conditioned to believe, through upbringing, habit, and culture, that we can only have so much health and happiness, and even so much awareness and consciousness. That stress and pain are to be expected and tolerated.

It is possible to change our set-point, or what we settle for, or our set way of looking at and labeling events in our lives.

Our standards and values drive whether and how we take a stand for our health and well-being. When we value self-care, preventive maintenance, and fulfillment, we are more ready to recognize that we may be settling for unhealthy conditions. When we value indulgence, quick solutions, and poor environmental practices, we are more apt to settle for less.

Our culture and economy—such as in the field of health care—has placed a greater emphasis on fixing problems than on preventing them. As a result, we have come to rely on or expect to be rescued by the fix (through a pill, the emergency medical team, or an insurance benefit). This, rather than take accountability for our own lives. We can be true self-leaders through a healthy lifestyle and healthy coping habits.

By itself, the map of different stress levels that I present here has no use. But it can be very helpful when seen as a tool for identifying your set-point, for tapping into your raw coping power, and for valuing prevention and self-care. As with any other map, it is useful for planning and traveling across the terrain. Here, the terrain is your own transformation.

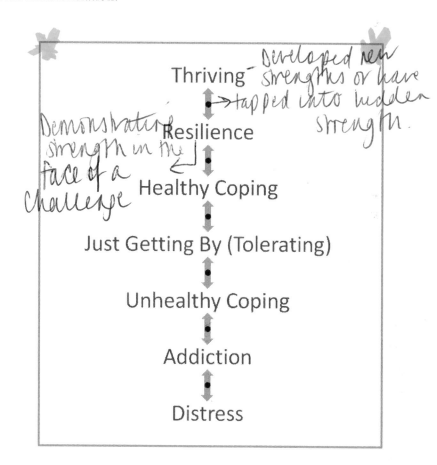

Thriving — *Developed new strengths or have → tapped into hidden strength.*

*Demonstrating strength in the ← face of a challenge*

Resilience

Healthy Coping

Just Getting By (Tolerating)

Unhealthy Coping

Addiction

Distress

The labels we apply for these levels are distress, addiction, unhealthy coping, just getting by (tolerating), healthy coping, resilience, and thriving. Our raw coping power gives us the strength to move from stress (distress) to resilience and thriving.

It is always a choice to move up or down a level. Our environment can have a strong influence on that choice and, with severe trauma, we may need external support over a period of time to change our set-point.

The bi-directional arrow between each level conveys that our set-point is rarely stuck or fixated at only one point; we are always moveable. In any given day, we fluctuate depending upon changes in our situation: daily hassles and daily uplifts, our attitude, energy, lifestyle habits, traffic, boss's mood, workload, and so on.

The idea of levels is meant to show that we are inclined to hang out for an extended period at one level or between levels. This is where values are important because they tend to be more enduring than day-to-day changes.

In my experience as a trainer, asking participants about their values is often the most effective way to make them aware of their set-point. I ask: "Has there been an event in your life—a crisis, trauma, or major change—that led you to realize you needed to change the way you lived? Did life ever give you a wake-up call?" Very often, this question reveals what is most important and can lead to a shift in your set-point.

One of the tools in the tool chapter asks you to review those values that motivate you to take better care of yourself. In actuality, this may not be valuing health as much as valuing family or personal growth. Each of us has our own unique value pattern. We each must find our own inner compass and, within that, the energy that points the arrow of that compass in the exceptionable direction of our own fulfillment.

In order to cultivate your raw coping power, you will need to ask yourself if you are really living your values. Are your behaviors expressing what is important to you? Do you need a wake-up call?

Social groups of all kinds can engage in awareness-raising
processes, help others tap into their raw coping power, and
together transform stress into an experience of thriving at
the group, organizational, and even cultural levels.

As LONG AS CULTURAL CONDITIONS communicate that fixing problems
is more important than preventing them, and social norms focus on
teaching individual or "self-help" skills for stress management, then
individuals may wrongly believe that their stress levels are completely
due to their own skills or lack thereof. But we know that environmental and social conditions play a large and often more important role
than individual skills alone.

This is why social groups will also benefit by using concepts and
skills to transform cultural conditions. We all benefit from social
norms that support prevention, health, well-being, resilience, and
thriving. A higher level of health and consciousness in a group can
provide the conditions necessary to promote growth in individuals
within the group.

The following points may aid social groups (teams, workplaces,
families) in their quest to transform stress into experiences of
thriving.

Similar to individuals, groups and organizations also have a set-
point for the well-being/joy (thriving) versus the disease/pain (distress) thresholds they are willing to tolerate as a group. For example,

if one individual in the group gets "too happy" or "too successful," there may be social pressure for that person to conform to a lower level of health or success.[4]

In one supervisor training I provided, a new supervisor was concerned about a deviant work practice of a particular employee. The other supervisors at the training had already dealt with this one "bad apple." They not only had given up but were now encouraging the new manager to ignore the problem, saying things like, "Let it go. He's not worth the trouble. He'll always find a way to get away with stuff."

This set-point also places an upper limit on experience. As individuals in a group become healthier and have experiences that challenge the norm, they may have difficulty "being heard." The rest of the group may simply ignore new messages or may even label, judge, reject, or stigmatize that individual who is raising his or her set-point. This occurs in the areas of physical and mental health.

For example, a coworker who has lost weight may be stigmatized for not joining in when others bring elaborate birthday cakes. In another case, I worked with one client where everyone knew that a married manager in one department was having an affair with an employee in another department. Everyone made a silent agreement to not say anything despite the fact that the relationship dynamics created anxiety and emotional stress for many. My client would try to talk about this to her coworkers, but they all ignored her.

> We can act to "be heard" or settle for just being part of "the herd." Which groups do you belong to that support your voice of awareness?

A goal of all the material and tools in this manual is to raise awareness so that we can all choose a higher upper limit, at the individual, group, family, and organizational level.

Our response to stressors—as individuals and as groups—is influenced by the set-point and other factors we are not conscious of. Some of those factors may be early childhood training, unwritten rules from our family or culture, previous unresolved trauma, and deeply held belief systems that we have never examined.

We can become conscious and make better choices that follow health-giving values and tap into our raw coping power. That's the point of this book.

Addictive processes (food, substances, compulsion, enabling, workaholism, and adrenaline addiction, for example) are a major factor in keeping us unaware of many of the processes discussed in this book.[5] This includes lack of consciousness about stressors, our own strain, our values, and our set-point. In general, a consumer-based culture and related marketing tends to support addictive processes. Examples include the architecture of a grocery store that places unhealthy foods more at eye-level or the ever-present candy selection at the checkout line.

Both addictive and awareness-raising processes occur in individuals, groups, and organizations. By addictive processes I refer to any tendency in an organization to dismiss or deny that problems exist or operate out of fear to protect money, job security, or an organizational image. Consider the previous example where no one was willing to speak up or rock the boat because they were afraid to jeopardize their jobs.

Alternately, many organizations have systems in place to raise awareness about problems. One example is the National Health Service in Great Britain that posts and disseminates examples of individual employees who have been subject to discrimination or bullying and who, as whistle-blowers, have been compensated for their difficulties.[6]

Stress and resilience are but single threads taken from the broadly
woven cloth of the human experience of challenge. In our quest to
meet challenge, we can use energy to go beyond resilience and
show audacity—experiencing conversion, peak experiences,
flourishing, or thriving.

STRESS IS ONE CHOICE IN A SELECTION of experiences that includes
thriving, resilience, and audacity. Audacity means extraordinary
boldness, bringing zest and energy to one's life, calling, or destiny.

Consider life as a multiple choice test. Do you choose

(A) I boldly "seize the day,"

(B) I go with the flow,

(C) I just let things happen as they happen, or

(D) I act like a victim of circumstance?

Life is a rich experience that includes both adversity and positive
uplifts. We do not always know, from one day to another, what circumstance may challenge our current level of health. As Forrest
Gump so aptly said, "Life is like a box of chocolates. You never know
what you are going to get."

Select a chocolate from an assortment and bite into it. You may
get something you like or something you are less fond of. Caramels,
nougats, toffees, coconuts, truffles, creams, nuts, fruits, crisps, and
jellies. Possibilities. Not everything is predictable. There is novelty.
We get much more from discovering than from seeking to control life.

To expand the metaphor, let's look at some other possible chocolates. Note that five of these six bring positive or upward energy. The odds are in our favor.[7]

*Adversity:* An experience of loss, failure, disease, or negative challenge that typically results in distress and a temporary lowering of your set-point.

*Resilience:* An experience of bouncing back from adversity, where the set-point returns to its previous, and higher, level of functioning.

*Thriving:* An experience of responding to adversity or any type of challenge that leads to a raising of your set-point beyond the level of resilience, at least for an extended period and even in the presence of continued or new challenges.

*Peak Experience:* A temporary experience that radically lifts your level of functioning beyond normal levels of consciousness.

*Conversion:* An experience that permanently changes your set-point. Typically, a religious, mystical experience (for example, you have a life-changing vision).

*Flourishing:* Sustained experience of cycles of increased functioning beyond a level of healthy coping, where new challenges result in increased functioning. For example, you get a new job that is such a great fit for your talents that your colleagues show increasing admiration; you're given harder challenges that you embrace, and you end up rising to the top of the organization in record time. Yes, this does happen!).

The following diagrams show how these different experiences work over time (the horizontal or left-to-right axis) to impact your health or functioning (the vertical or up-and-down axis). The set-point is described by the dashed line. Again, our set-point represents our set way of looking at events.

For example, the first diagram shows that adversity tends to lower our level of functioning, while resilience helps us to bounce back to our previous level of functioning or expected set-point. But the second diagram shows that we can learn so much from the challenge that we exceed our previous set-point. This is one definition of thriving.

## Six Types of Experiences That Make Life Rich

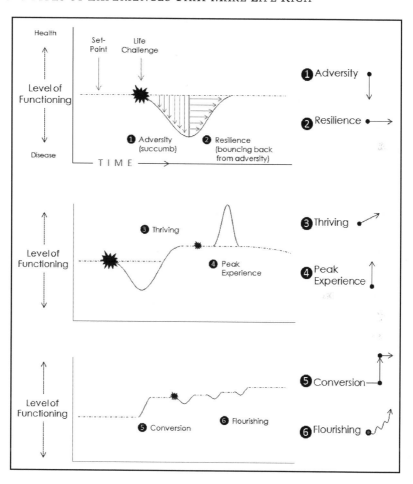

The graphs above view our level of functioning (from disease to health) on the vertical axis and time on the horizontal axis. Our set-point or set way of being is represented by the dashed line and can remain relatively stable, decrease (from adversity) and recover (with resilience); exceed its original level (thriving); have a rapid increase (peak experience); change permanently (conversion); or go through cycles of increase (flourishing). The direction of energy varies across these six different ways of experiencing life.

When we fail to stop stress in its tracks, mind-body contractions can lead to disease, depression, and other problems. The good news is that our nervous system is a well-oiled feedback system, allowing us to deal with stress at every stage. By doing so, we can reverse the progression of stress and turn it into an experience of resilience or thriving.

STRESS DOES NOT HAPPEN ALL AT ONCE. It progresses in stages. Our brain, nervous, and immune systems are perfectly designed to receive feedback and respond to stress at each stage. To respond effectively, we may need only to apply careful attention and a loving attitude of ease and self-care. Reflect on how you might process each stage of stress awareness as you follow the examples in each stage

*Stage 1: Stressor Awareness.* You identify a situation, event, thought, feeling, or mental state and evaluate it as potentially harmful. You may then take action to alleviate the harm. If not, you may then start to experience strain (and move to Stage 2).

Example: You become aware that your direct supervisor is applying pressure on you to work longer hours that you never agreed to as part of your terms of hire. You are uncomfortable but don't know what to do. To use the metaphor from weather, the clouds are gathering and it is starting to rain.

*Stage 2: Early Warning Signs.* We each experience strain differently. I give some examples here. Catching these signs in time will allow you to act to reduce them.

Physical: You may experience headaches, hypertension, stomach problems, immune deficiency such as in catching colds more easily, muscle tension, asthma, or exhaustion.

Emotional: You might feel anxious, angry, irritable, frustrated, or excitable.

Mental: You might have increased distractibility or impaired concentration or reasoning.

Social: You may find yourself being grouchy, impulsive, critical, hostile, complaining, oversensitive, or snappy.

You may have any combination of these signs.

Example: As a result of the job pressure to work late, you have headaches and anxiety and are grouchy at home. A perfect storm is brewing.

*Stage 3: Tolerance Awareness.* Failing to deal with your warning signs (as listed in Stage 2), you can begin to tolerate the stress. You settle upon the belief and tell yourself, *These are just the way things are.* At this stage, some of us tend to remain outwardly calm under stress, while others among us feel dissonance or tension. In other words, we are tolerating a situation that goes against our values (for example, our values about self-care). Here, we are being challenged to be audacious: do the right thing and address the situation.

Example: You start paying attention to the job pressure and your own symptoms and realize that they are connected. You realize that you have been tolerating your supervisor because you have not been willing to take any action. Now you are feeling a reduction in your own well-being. It might be time to get out the umbrella.

*Stage 4: Engage Coping Mechanisms.* This stage may occur before or after any of the previous stages to deal with the source of stress, strain, or tolerance. Coping mechanisms can be healthy and effective or unhealthy and ineffective. Effective coping is preventive and typically reduces stress exposure, alleviates strain, and creates healthy tolerance of situations. Ineffective coping does the opposite.

Example: When the headaches first start coming on, you resort to taking a pain reliever several times a day, drinking coffee, and on occasion going out to happy hour with some coworkers. These actions are ineffective.

Later, as your tolerance awareness increases, you begin to draft a plan about how you will communicate with your supervisor and let him know how his pressure is not working. You feel better by just having and working on this plan and gathering the information you need to defend yourself. You not only have the umbrella deployed but you have all the weather gear assembled in case you need to travel into the storm at a moment's notice.

At a biological level, Stage 3 and Stage 4 represent the work of our body's immune system. When our bodies are invaded by foreign germs, an alarm may sound that alerts the immune system, warning of a potential disease. At that point, a healthy immune system knows what it can and cannot tolerate. If the tolerance level is exceeded, the immune response is activated.

*Stage 5: Later Warning Signs.* This stage results when the previous stages have not been effective. Later warning signs include burnout, withdrawal from others, depression, post-traumatic stress disorder when the stress involves exposure to particular kinds of trauma, chronic anxiety, chronic addiction, and other known stress-related diseases (such as cardiovascular and immunological problems like high cholesterol or an increased amount of cold sores and sore throats).

Even at this stage it is possible to apply the previous tools, but I strongly recommend that you reach out for professional help. Getting professional help is one of the best stress management skills available.

People don't reach out for help for many reasons, and the tools in this book can help to address many of them. For example, people are either in denial about the problem or simply are unaware that help is available. They may also believe it is a sign of weakness or that others will not think of them as strong. Also, many work cultures do not support taking time for self-help.

In one study, we found that employees in organizations that had higher work stress were actually less likely to contact their employee assistance programs (EAP) in comparison with employees in organizations with less stress who gladly worked closely with the EAP.[8]

Example: Imagine that instead of drafting a plan you just continued to tolerate the situation. Eventually your headaches, anxiety, and unhappy behavior at home, along with your ineffective coping would start to wear on you and your relationships with others. Moreover, because of strong social norms at work you never realize that there is an EAP nor enough time to get help anyway. You end up depressed. Those dark clouds linger for a long time.

> Just the will to flourish—to optimistically envision growth and goodness coming from your good works—is enough to interrupt the progression of stress in an instant.

What is the key take-away from knowing these five stages? The main point is that we have the ability to pause, exercise awareness of the progression, and choose an effective response. This awareness tends to require less effort at earlier rather than later stages. Either way, we don't have to "go on automatic" and, like a machine, inevitably have stress result in Stage 5 warning signs. In fact, we can even catch ourselves at that stage and reverse the damage the stress has caused. This ability to reverse damage has even been documented in cancer patients.

CANCER RECOVERY[9]

The story of Kris Carr is but one, albeit popular, example of how a cancer patient can thrive with cancer. At age thirty-one, she was diagnosed with an incurable form of liver cancer. She considered this a wake-up call and began searching for natural solutions. She writes:

> *I learned that a nutrient dense, plant-passionate diet rules,*
> *the Standard American Diet destroys (everything), stress*
> *sucks (all life force), exercise is non-negotiable (great for your*
> *head, heart, cells and ass-ets), joy is utterly contagious, and*
> *having fun must be taken very seriously.*

Kris documented her transformation in the movie *Crazy, Sexy, Cancer* (2007) and has served as an inspiration to thousands of people who look to prevent or recover from cancer. Check out kriscarr.com.

Kris's story is not unique. Many stories of tumors vanishing and other cancer remissions point to the important role of conscious intention as a key to raw coping power. My colleague, Bill Baun, has repeatedly witnessed these stories as Wellness Director for the MD Anderson Cancer Center: "I've taught, coached, and counseled individuals and groups about the body-mind-spirit connections and I've heard amazing stories about individuals uncovering their inner strengths. They find ways to get back to just being ... and thriving."

## A Summary of The 7 Basic Principles

1 ▪ We are designed to learn so much so that we deliberately place ourselves in stressful situations for the purpose of growth and transformation.

2 ▪ We can systematically transform our approach to stress from "the kiss of death" to "the spice of life."

3 ▪ We each have an innate or in-born raw coping power; we can tap into this and work with stress as part of our own transformation.

4 ▪ Our values determine the level through which we process stress, from severe distress to a rich uplifting experience of thriving.

5 ▪ Social groups can help others tap into their raw coping power and together transform stress into an experience of thriving at the cultural level.

6 ▪ We can go beyond resilience and show audacity in our quest for conversion, peak experiences, flourishing, or thriving.

7 ▪ Our nervous system is a well-oiled feedback system that allows us to deal with stress at every stage.

### USING THE SEVEN PRINCIPLES WITH OTHERS

What if the workplace, community or culture you live in does not support these principles?

It is likely that our social systems do not support the basic idea that we can transform stress into a positive resource. These systems lag behind the science of resilience, thriving, and transformation. It is important to understand, rather than blame, these systems because we ourselves have a hand in creating them. Most often, those who lead or manage our communities and organizations are themselves blind to context and system-level influences I have been discussing.

They tolerate things like the rest of us. They believe that their set-point is inflexible. They ignore their own personal stress warning signs. They forget their values and underestimate the role of the environment. Executives and politicians as well as local leaders and those in any organization or association we belong to all need our help. They have a choice.

Not everyone will agree with the claim that stress is a choice. This claim must be qualified in at least three situations where choice can be limited. First, prolonged or severe exposure to stressors or trauma such as a childhood of abuse, war, imprisonment, extreme isolation, or repeated exposure to harassment or violence. Second, living or working in environments that provide people with severely limited control, variety, or freedom (a job on an assembly line could be in this category). Third, inherited institutions or ways of doing things, often in place for many years or even generations, and governed by strict rules that require adherence under threat of rejection, stigmatization, or punishment are stress producing.

Examples of the latter exist in any country or people that has been persecuted or discriminated against. This includes the persecution of Christians in the Roman Empire, Jews in Eastern Europe during the Holocaust, and African-Americans prior to full implementation of the Civil Rights Act.

These types of stressors may be respectively labeled as trauma, imprisonment, and consensual trance, and each limit our choices. Still, both history and science bear witness to the fact that in each of the situations, people, groups, and societies can raise their set-point, transform the situation, and thrive.

Consider the set-point again:

But this time, imagine that with every stressful situation you have a choice based on your tendencies and values as follows:

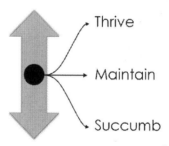

There are core models of stress, informed by scientific research, which clearly show that we have the ability to resist succumbing and can move from maintaining to thriving. The next chapter reviews these ways or lenses of looking at stress. They give you a "big picture" so you can prevent system blindness. They can be handy to remember if you ever come to doubt the seven basics.

Therefore, this book is a "research to practice" guide that helps you and others you work or live with. We cannot sit around and wait for these systems to change. It is only through our own efforts (usually as a team and community) that we can change these systems. In fact, the lack of community may be the most important reason for our increased vulnerability to stress in the modern world.

The next chapter provides a wide lens—actually ten different lenses—for talking about and working with stress in a transformative way, at the individual and group or community level.

Again, these models have some support from research, which is documented at the end of this book for those who want to read more. The models are good to know. However, knowing these models will not be enough. As the saying goes: "People don't care how much you know, unless they also know how much you care." By adopting these lenses, you can begin to show such care for yourself. Further, these lenses prepare you for the tools in the final chapter of the book. These tools can and should be used with others as a way to shift systems in a positive direction.

> Right now, can you bring to mind someone you are grateful for? Can you kindle a spark that grows into a thriving community?

# | 2 |

# The 10 Different Lenses

HERE ARE TEN DIFFERENT WAYS TO VIEW stress (I call them lenses) to help you cope with stress in a transformative way. This chapter looks at each lens in preparation for the next chapter that shows you how to use the lenses with tools to tap into your raw coping power.

The lenses represent different ways of viewing the world and the role of stress in your world. They are intended to give you--and your brain--a sense that there are many different perspectives through which you can approach the challenges you face, alone and together with your community (family, workplace).

> 1 ▪ *Stressor-Strain:* While stressors can lead to strain and health problems, we can prevent stress from having a negative impact.
>
> 2 ▪ *Post-Traumatic Growth:* We can grow from adversity and trauma, learning to both heal and thrive from trauma.
>
> 3 ▪ *Neuroplasticity:* Our brain is designed for resilience and thriving through inner connections with ourselves and outer connections with community.

4 ▪ *Potentiation:* Stress holds a great potential that we can leverage for the purpose of meaning, growth, and fulfillment.

5 ▪ *Team Resilience:* Five resilience competencies can be cultivated in all individuals and social groups: Centering, Community, Compassion, Confidence, and Commitment.

6 ▪ *Positive Coping Cycle:* We each have an inner guardian—an evaluator—who stands between our stressors and our strain and selects effective coping strategies.

7 ▪ *Negative Coping Cycle:* We can develop ineffective coping habits that place ourselves at risk for addiction.

8 ▪ *Team Awareness:* Our local social connections and the social environment influence our choice between positive and negative coping.

9 ▪ *Manager Pathways for Potentiation:* Leaders can develop, harness, and potentiate the positive stress cycle.

10 ▪ *The We in Wellness:* Being part of the *we* in wellness may be the necessary trigger for raising our set-point and both choosing and maintaining a healthy lifestyle.

"Every adversity, every failure, and every heartache carries with it the seed of an equivalent or greater benefit."

—Napolean Hill

*The Stressor-Strain Model* [1]

Scientists have tended to view stress through "the problem" lens.
They emphasize the stressor and its inevitable impact on strain.
This viewpoint has helped establish stress as a cause of many
types of problems in health and productivity. It has also
helped to identify factors (buffers) that can either stop
stress or lessen its negative impact.

THIS MODEL FOLLOWS THE CLASSICAL NOTION in physics of cause-and-effect and the ideas of force and momentum. There is an event, often described in negative terms (adversity). That event has a force, which means that it will propel something in a certain direction. Unless some factor impedes, slows down, or re-directs the energy of that force, the stress will have an impact on health.

This model tends to view the individual, organization, or social system as a passive processor of stress. It is as though scientists have said: "Let's first understand what stress is, how it works, and measure its impact." Rather than: "Let's understand how human systems are designed to process stress" and, even better, "Let's examine their capacity for preventing or transforming it."

As a result of this way of seeing things—often called a paradigm—our language tends to focus on de-stressing, or managing rather than transforming stress. It is important to note that the idea of transformation also exists in physics and other areas such as engineering, mathematics, and music. We can learn from these areas. [2]

In one example from music, the composer Franz Liszt developed a method of transforming themes in a musical composition. Composers can transform a particular series of notes over and over again in a musical work. This basic theme is repeated in a variety of ways: disguised, fragmented, reassembled, enhanced or diminished, contrasted or merged with other note sequences.

In a parallel way, we can imagine that stress is its own series of notes. We may only need to learn how to be creative with it. While it is a fixed paradigm, the stressor-strain lens has been very useful in a number of ways. For example, it has helped identify factors that buffer the negative impact of stress on health. Buffering factors include personality traits, education, intelligence, and various stress management skills. Social support is perhaps the most well-established buffer. [3] It greatly helps to have others in our lives who care about us and whom we care about in creating a sense of community or strong positive social bonds. Love and friendship can reduce, alleviate, or actively stop the adverse impact of stress on health.

Despite its usefulness, this lens has some drawbacks. For example, it focuses on individuals, rather than on environments or systems, as responsible for handling stress. It also assumes a linear or single arrow: cause (stressor)-and-effect (strain); if the buffer factors don't intervene, then strain is inevitable. It tends to look at the final end state as either strain or some level of alleviating strain. That is, stress is defined as a negative from beginning to end. Finally, there is no feedback to the individual as a result of their learning from all the stages of stress.

*Post-Traumatic Growth*

Post-traumatic growth is one of the best indicators that raw coping power is real and commonplace. Just as our skin grows back after a cut or a bone re-knits after a break, we each have the ability to mend following a severely stressful event or situation. And we can learn specific factors that promote recovery and afford healing.

TRAUMA IS DEFINED AS A SPECIFIC TYPE of adversity. In medicine, the focus is on a physical wound to the body caused by an external source. In psychology or psychiatry, trauma is an emotional response to a terrible event such as a disaster, violence, abuse or neglect. This emotional response includes shock, denial, unpredictable emotions, flashbacks, strained relationships, and physical symptoms.

Science in both medicine and mental health, has clearly established the phenomenon known as post-traumatic growth.[4] Clinical studies show how people recover from, and grow after, a wide variety of traumatic experiences including earthquakes, terrorism attacks, accidents, breast cancer, and heart attacks. Medicine also documents how bone and tissue re-grows and re-forms after trauma injury or a transplant.

In short, human beings are innately wired—both in body and mind—to recover and experience positive changes as a result of severely stressful events. Positive psychological changes that have been documented include an increased appreciation for life, setting of new life priorities, a sense of increased personal strength, identification of new possibilities, improved closeness in intimate relationships, or positive spiritual change.

A number of factors determine post-traumatic growth, its levels, and sustainment over time. Here are some of them:

- Having experienced early adversity before rather than living a protected or pampered life. This is like the saying: *What doesn't kill us makes us stronger.*[5]
- Adopting a positive outlook (optimism, hope) when interpreting different events. *When all you have is lemons, make lemonade.*
- Being willing to keep moving in a positive direction, especially after initial setbacks. A quote from F. Scott Fitzgerald explains: *Vitality shows in not only the ability to persist but in the ability to start over.*
- Being willing to have positive emotions, despite the gravity of the situation. Having insight and understanding that our emotions can be complex. *It's not the end of the world!*
- Having a sense of hardiness or self-determination. To paraphrase the scientist Maxwell Maltz: *We maintain our balance, poise, and sense of security only by moving forward.*

WHOLE FOODS MARKET: AN ORGANIZATIONAL EXAMPLE OF POST-TRAUMATIC GROWTH [6]

Currently, Whole Foods Market is a grocery chain dedicated to providing health and whole foods, with over 370 stores and 80,000 employees located throughout the United States. A pivotal moment in the history of Whole Foods occurred within one year of formally opening their first store in 1980. As their website reports:

On Memorial Day in 1981, the worst flood in 70 years devastated the city of Austin. Caught in the flood waters, the store's inventory was wiped out and most of the equipment was damaged. The losses were approximately $400,000 and Whole Foods Market had no insurance. Customers and neighbors voluntarily joined the staff to repair and clean up the damage. Creditors, vendors and investors all provided breathing room for the store to get back on its feet and it re-opened only 28 days after the flood.

A key part of this event was how it affected its CEO and founder, John Mackey. In an interview with Billionaire, he recalls: "The store was eight feet under water, everything was destroyed and we had no insurance or savings. We would've died if everyone had not rallied around us."

In many ways, this event opened Mackey's eyes to the importance of all stakeholders, of compassion, and of the spirit of community. Employees, customers, suppliers, investors, and the banker all believed enough in the mission of Whole Foods to chip in and help and not let the store die. Here is an excerpt from Mackey's interview with KERA television in Dallas.

> *The things that are the most challenging are the things you learn most from ... This was the beginning of my understanding of stakeholders and how important they are to the company. You just don't exist to make money for your investors. I realized that our stakeholders love us and I have always felt passionate about our stakeholders ever since then. It changed my life and the way I think about business.*

This story shows the transformative power of adversity, a key part of the lens on post-traumatic growth. Mackey is now the co-author of several books on conscious capitalism, which extends the story of collaboration with stakeholders as a whole new and enlightened way of doing business.

## Neuroplasticity

The brain is designed for resilience and thriving. This design
involves connections within ourselves—our coherent sense of self as
a social being. We have to connect ourselves with ourselves (tune in)
and with others—through compassion (to self and others) and
through community (reaching out and receiving help).

BRAIN SCIENCE HAS SHOWN US that we rewire our brains when we
learn new tasks. We expand the links between our brain cells (neu-
rons), form new "neural networks," and create different neural pathways that did not exist prior to such learning.

Neuroplasticity, as the dictionary defines it, is the capacity of neu-
rons and neural networks to change their connections and behavior
in response to new information, sensory stimulation, development,
damage, or dysfunction.[7]

Research shows that positive emotional and socially connecting
experiences can increase neurochemicals that foster neuroplasticity.
By engaging in mental exercises, social interactions, contemplative
or mindful techniques, and using tools for well-being, we can improve our mind-body health just as engaging in physical exercise and
healthy diet improves our physical health.

The phenomenon of neuroplasticity also suggests that we can re-
learn/re-pattern previously set-up patterns or routines. It is possible

to teach an old dog new tricks, to revisit previous harmful memories, to recast and learn from them, and to recover from long-term unhealthy habits and addictions. We can change our set-point.

The key ingredient in neuroplasticity is connectivity, in contrast to segmenting or walling off one aspect of our brain from another. There is evidence of reduced connectivity between the right and left hemispheres among those who experience more adversity. Those who respond better to negative events have more connectivity between the brain's emotional and higher-reasoning circuits.

Most importantly, connectivity at the neural level has a parallel at the experiential level in the form of compassion.[8] It appears that neuroplasticity is nurtured when we connect with another's emotional experience and have and show feelings of care and empathy. Social support might be the key buffer between stress and strain because it provides the opportunity for helping, altruism, and compassion.

Some may label this "tribal resilience," a capacity deeply wired into our species. One that has (literally and figuratively) *helped* us survive and thrive throughout evolution.

*Potentiation*

Seeing the potential value within stressors and strains, we act to draw out that potential with confidence, leadership, optimism, hope, resiliency, self-determination, and hardiness. We mobilize these resources by seeing stress as an opportunity for achieving meaning, growth, and fulfillment.

THE STRESSOR-STRAIN LENS SHOWS us how stressors lead to strain. We respond to challenge and adversity with the goal of alleviating stress and strain. In contrast, with the potentiation view, we proactively "take on" stress. Challenges lead us to mobilize internal resources for the goals of growth, meaning-making, learning, and self-awareness.

This lens differs from the previous ones. Instead of relieving stress as the goal, potentiation begins with growth or wisdom as the end in mind. Our experiences provide the groundwork for maturation. We have distinct resources (and I'll list those next) to leverage stress, trauma, negative experiences, hardships, or challenges; to mine the hidden gold in them; to "milk" them for their value; to draw out their potential for the purpose of growth and even radical growth and innovation.

Life events provide us with feedback to help us continue to discover meaning. We may need to listen and to practice acceptance—even a radical acceptance—to see the potential in that feedback.

The following resources represent different lines of research on potentiation.[10]

*Efficacy:* Confidence in being able to produce a desired result.

*Psychological capital:* Having optimism, hope, resilience, and efficacy.

*Self-leadership:* We keep learning how to achieve the self-direction and self-motivation necessary to perform, do well, and obtain our goals. Self-leadership often involves some form of discipline (self-regulation, self-control).

*Self-determination:* We are motivated from within, by interests, curiosity, care, or abiding values. These intrinsic motivations are activated and supported by a sense of freedom, competence, and relatedness or connection to others.

*Hardiness:* Seeing life as a challenge, having a sense of control, and being willing to commit or persevere in the face of challenge.

*Flourishing and thriving:* While discussed elsewhere in this book, research shows that people with mental health problems or in recovery (such as alcoholism, depression, or schizophrenia) can still flourish in life even with their ongoing problems.

*Collective efficacy:* By coordinating or working with others, we build a sense of group confidence that the group can achieve desired results.

*Team resilience:* Resilience can exist at the team level, with each person bringing his or her own competency in one of these areas: Centering (stress management), Confidence, Commitment, Compassion, Community.

These are indeed a rich set of resources that, when we use them, multiply our potential to be healthy, productive, and successful. That is why this lens is called potentiation. For example, in one clinical study with Team Resilience training, we assessed employees' stress and productivity levels one year after they received some of the tools in this book. Importantly, we also assessed employees who never received the tools directly from us. They only worked in the same location as those who did or were hired months after the training. We found that even these new and untrained workers had reduced stress and less exposure to counterproductivity.[11]

What does this mean? Apparently, the program created a way for the message and tools to be carried forward or diffused into the work setting. This capacity then gave new employees greater potential to learn how to manage their stress. In addition, those who received the tools became more competent at transforming stress and subsequently role-modeled this behavior to others. Other locations with employees who did not have the training still had exposure to stress. These employees did not demonstrate the same ability to cope with the new stressors they faced.

"Where you stumble, there lies your treasure. The very cave you are afraid to enter turns out to be the source of what you are looking for."

— Joseph Campbell

## Five Competencies of Resilience: A Synthesis

Here's a simple way to remember the seven "basics" and the
previous lenses. These five competencies of resilience exist in
individuals, teams, and organizations: Centering, Community,
Compassion, Confidence, and Commitment.

REMEMBER THAT RESILIENCE IS ONE of the six experiences that enriches
life. It is that period when we bounce back from a low point of adversity and return to our set-point. Although resilience is only one of the six
experiences, there is something deeply moving, life-giving, and even
awe-inspiring when we see or meet someone who has overcome trage-
dy, life-threatening situations, or shown courage under fire.

Yes, our notions of heroism are woven together with resilience.
The underlying driver of resilience—our raw coping power—also
lives in social groups or teams. Teams can also be our heroes. We pay
great cultural attention to the development, competition, and cele-
bration of teams. This occurs in almost every area of life, for example,
in sports, business and the arts, not to mention service projects such
as Habitat for Humanity.

Five competencies comprise resilience and resilient teams.[12]
Rarely does a single team member have all five. On any team, one
member will usually show enough of one competency to make a positive
impact on team performance and health. Each member has something
to give, to appreciate in others, and to complement the team.

*Centering (Coping)* includes a healthy lifestyle, wellness, diet, moderation, exercise; using stress management skills; faith, spiritual health; work-life balance.

*Community (Care)* includes social connection, positive group activities that foster social capital; giving and getting help; knowing how to refer others to helpful resources (family or peer referral).

*Compassion (Character)* entails having active empathy for others and their hardships; virtues of heart-centered leadership: integrity, authenticity, humility; character strength and cultivating a moral compass.

*Confidence (Control)* provides a positive self-focus, embracing and enjoying challenge; also knowing one's limits, having self-control, and courage.

*Commitment (Calling)* means following one's goals and dreams; clarifying direction and purpose; planning and organizing to achieve goals; persevering and persisting in the face of obstacles to one's goals.

*The Positive Coping Cycle:*
*Stress → Evaluate → Cope*

We can strengthen an inner guardian to stand between our
stressors and our strain. This guardian evaluates situations, draws
upon a multitude of positive resources, and selects effective coping
strategies. To strengthen this guardian, we practice a
healthy lifestyle and centering skills.

WE CAN APPLY THE PREVIOUS POSITIVE factors to the Stressor-Strain
Model: post-traumatic growth, neuroplasticity, potentiation, and resilience. These factors live between the stress and the strain, causing
us to cope effectively. When we follow a healthy lifestyle and practice
daily centering skills, each of these stands like a sturdy guardian between the stressor and the strain, leading us to thrive and flourish.

Remember the five stages: stressor awareness, early warning
signs, tolerance awareness, coping, and later warning signs. At each
stage we can slow down, pause, take a breath, and reflect on our situation. We can evaluate what is happening to us. In highly stressful,
life-threatening situations, this evaluation can take less than a second. For most circumstances of our life, we have time—if only a few
minutes—during the day to stop and evaluate.

So first there is the stressor. Then there is the step to evaluate the
kind of centered and compassionate attentiveness that leads to clari-

ty and discernment. And with effective evaluation, there is effective coping. Most of the tools I provide in the next chapter of this book assist with evaluation, to strengthen your inner guardian.

You may use two sets of tools. First, a healthy lifestyle that includes daily exercise; a healthy plant-based diet free of processed foods, fats, and sugars; adequate sleep and rest; time devoted to personal reflection, meditation, or prayer; and opportunities for positive social connection, good conversation, giving and sharing support.

> Evaluate your situation: a centered and compassionate attentiveness that brings clarity and discernment.

Second, we also need to distinguish between and support effective versus ineffective coping strategies. Effective coping strategies include connecting with others, problem solving, positive self-talk, exercise, creativity, and taking time for reflection. Ineffective coping includes giving in to addictive tendencies, indulging, negative self-talk, avoiding situations, withdrawing from others, and zoning out with television, the Internet, and mindless games.

The next chapter provides exercises to help you better distinguish these strategies in your own life. But first, we must understand a process that can hurt your inner guardian, and that is the negative coping cycle.

## STRESS DRIVES ATTENTION: INWARD OR OUTWARD?

Stress energizes and mobilizes our mind-body system, saying "Pay Attention!" With the positive coping cycle, our attention tends to go inward to review possible alternative behaviors and their outcomes and then determine the best choice. This can happen in an instant. High-performing athletes—especially in competitive sports—thrive on this type of stress; they have well-trained evaluation systems that really "take a sec" (or less than a second) to make the decision.

But stress can drive attention inward at a deeper and spiritual level. Think about significant life events such as the loss of a loved one, a major failure, being subject to war, poverty, or a catastrophe. Sometimes life brings us to our knees and makes us humble. Many people begin a life of spiritual devotion in response to these life-changing events. This may be a sudden religious conversion, but it may also be a gradual awakening that had its inception with a trauma.

Compare the positive coping cycle with the negative coping cycle. You may note that the positive inward focus enhances the possibility of high performance (as with athletes) and spiritual health. In contrast, the negative cycle's outward focus tends to distance us away from our innate capacities. We look outside ourselves for answers only to find temporary release or a "high" that does not serve our growth in the long run.

## The Negative Coping Cycle: Tension Release

Some life events are too painful to evaluate. Or we develop habits
to help release tension and pursue pleasure to help offset the pain.
As a result, we avoid the positive coping cycle and place ourselves
at risk for addiction. The outcomes of our tension release can
produce their own stress, resulting in a negative cycle. The negative
cycle is a choice but one taken less often when we live in
a healthy connected community.

AS DESCRIBED EARLIER, WE CAN PROCESS stressful experiences at
different levels, from distress to thriving. One relatively low level
bears the label of addiction. Here our inner guardian requires great
vigilance. We must be on guard, especially when compulsive coping
habits become automatic, routine, and over-indulgent.

Addiction means that we get caught between a negative cycle of
distress and unhealthy coping, looking for an expedient way to re-
lieve tension, rather than evaluating our situation. When you become
addicted, life loses it richness. There is no resilience, thriving, or conversion. In fact, it can often take a strong conversion experience—a
wake-up call—to rouse our inner guardian and start back on the path
of raising our set-point.

Why does addiction happen? Different answers from science have
been tested and different solutions have been shown to work.[13] The
raw coping power perspective suggests that we don't stop long

enough or deeply enough to truly evaluate our situation, especially painful aspects of the stressful experience. Addiction happens, in part, because we believe it is too painful to assess the stress. Many who suffer severe trauma (as children or adults) can turn to drugs, alcohol, or other substances and processes as a way to either kill the pain or keep the restive demons of their past at bay.

Society also plays a role by how it fosters, normalizes, advertises, and provides access to addictive substances.[14] Consider fast food, foods that are highly processed and fatty, sugary foods (candy, doughnuts), tobacco, and alcohol. When these become increasingly and widely available, the result is obesity, lung cancer, and other problems (such as drunk driving and job-related alcohol impairment). Our society also exposes us to processes such as gambling, pornography, violence, and over-romanticized images of beauty. Each of these can be the basis for addiction.

Every day we can choose between the positive and negative coping cycle. By engaging in a healthy lifestyle, we raise our set-point and guard against addiction, even if we allow ourselves indulgences from time to time. But we also need the courage to make choices that support our values, rather than compulsive behaviors that simply distract. We need the courage to abstain and the wisdom to live in healthy communities, with compassionate people, who follow societal norms that foster resilience.

One wonderful aspect of the positive cycle is that when we pause to evaluate, when we look around for resources, we will see different communities around us—communities that support and empower health as well as recovery from addiction and foster healthy coping. This includes many types of 12-step groups located in nearly every community. We also see groups that sanction and enable addictive lifestyles, such as those seen in high-risk social cliques in high school and university settings, in gangs, and certain bars and social venues.

It is possible to choose between these two types of communities just as we can choose between the positive or negative coping cycles. I have known people who moved themselves and sometimes their families miles away from communities or who drove an extra hour a day to go to a recovery meeting or support group just so they would be exposed to the positive message. These efforts helped to save their lives.

## THE POSITIVE AND NEGATIVE COPING CYCLES

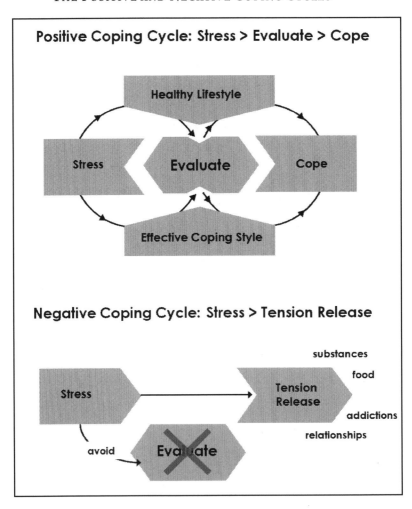

**Positive Coping Cycle: Stress > Evaluate > Cope**

Healthy Lifestyle

Stress | Evaluate | Cope

Effective Coping Style

**Negative Coping Cycle: Stress > Tension Release**

Stress

Tension Release

substances
food
addictions
relationships

avoid    Evaluate

*Team Awareness* [15]

Our social connections and the social environment shape our
choice between positive and negative coping. For any social group,
team, or family, there are core group practices to raise awareness and
help all team members move in the direction of positive coping.

NEGATIVE COPING AND ADDICTION are perhaps the most complex and
difficult challenges we can face. The negative coping cycle lies at the
root of many problems in health. People go on diets of all kinds only
to relapse because of stress. Nicotine addiction is fueled by stress.
And because work addiction can over-ride healthy lifestyles, a business that supports a workaholic lifestyle may never see a return on
investment from a wellness program.

It often takes a healthy team—with each member bringing his or
her own tools and talents—to deal with the complex and society-
based problems of addiction. It is possible to create a healthy team. In
fact, the future health of our families, our communities, and our
countries may depend on a renewal of real connection through
healthy teams. These teams would create a shared awareness and responsibility for problems of health that have previously been only
seen as an individual burden.

Through this team awareness in the workplace, employees openly
interact to create positive experiences solving problems together.
They can take actions to prevent the negative coping cycle. This idea

may seem radical. We typically think that individuals are responsible for problems of stress and addiction, for choosing health versus addiction, and for seeking help. But, as discussed, these choices are strongly influenced by social connections and the social environment.

Some core practices that empower team awareness include these:

- *Ask the team to create a motto, code of excellence, a logo or totem image that conveys their willingness to embrace principles described in this book.* For example, "We are willing to expand our capacity for greater health as a group" is a motto that can become part of a company's expressed goals. In one project, we worked with the National Electrical Contractor Association and International Brotherhood of Electrical Workers (NECA/IBEW). Their code of excellence helped set the tone of solid accountability for a high-risk and safety-sensitive occupation. One element in the code simply stated: "Work in a safe and healthy manner."

- *Educate the team on their own group risks and strengths by sharing the results of employee opinion surveys, or wellness, culture, or climate assessments.* The results then become the goals. In one agency we worked with, a large multi-employer survey revealed the importance of spending at least five hours a week relaxing with family at home. In comparison studies, workers who did not spend this time had higher stress at *both* work and at home. As a result, the agency sent out new media campaigns to help encourage more relaxation and also gave tips on how to get help for families struggling with time.

- *Invite employees to openly discuss the benefits of workplace policies as a way to make them aware that policy is a shared responsibility.* Especially if you wish to propose a new policy on, for example, drug testing. Wouldn't employee input early on help shape and strengthen a policy that employees can embrace? In fact, we worked with several companies that used Team Awareness prior to implementing drug testing as a way to communicate the importance of preventive stress management and help-seeking. Over and over again, the message "Get Help Before You Get Caught" has resulted in improved utilization of positive human resources.

- *Bring employees together to discuss how they would approach (hypothetical) counter-productive colleagues.* How much counter productivity would they tolerate? How can they communicate better and use resources to prevent counter-productive behaviors? Here's an example. We use an exercise in which employees work together in groups to discuss how much they would tolerate a coworker in different scenarios: (a) always comes to work late, (b) gossips about others and causes conflict at work, or (c) works with heavy machinery and is known to have a problem with alcohol use. These discussions often help to surface unspoken assumptions about roles and responsibilities. As a result, coworkers become more accountable to each other, which itself helps to reduce stress.

- *Provide fun and memorable ways to learn about health benefits, including the employee assistance program.* Reduce stigma for seeking help. We always create some type of competitive board game or a simple *Jeopardy*-type question-and-answer game. Teams answer a variety of questions about policy, benefits, and human resources along with other questions on health and stress. I am always heartened by how much fun employees have when they compete with each other and learn in the process. Such games provide an opportunity for collaboration and positive tension release in a group setting. This positive energy spills over into the work environment.

- *Promote communication, active listening, and respectful conversation skills.* There are many types of communication training available, and several can be found in the tools chapter.
- *Train employees to encourage each other with compassion.* We call this NUDGE (N=notice someone with stress; U=understand you have a role to play in helping them; D=decide if you should say something; G=use guidelines for effective communication; and E=encourage). The NUDGE model is presented in the next chapter.
- Provide *Raw Coping Power* training by sharing tools in this book.

---

MANY DIFFERENT VERSIONS OF TEAM AWARENESS

Through our consultation with Team Awareness, we have customized training in these core practices for different groups and cultures. The diversity of customization suggests that group awareness activities can be universally applied in all types of working groups. Some examples include these:

- In small businesses in construction, transportation, and service industries (see Small Business Wellness Initiative at www.sbwi.org)
- In nonprofit and community-oriented service agencies
- With Native American populations and tribal governments
- With ex-offenders who were part of a job retraining program
- With the military (The National Guard has adapted Team Readiness as a prevention program.)
- With municipalities in the United States and South Africa
- With electricians and electrician apprentices in union settings
- With high school and college youth in the Youth Conservation Corp
- With nursing students
- With young restaurant workers

---

*Manager Pathways for Potentiation*

Leaders or managers of groups are essential for developing and harnessing the positive stress cycle in the work setting. They only need to walk the talk in order to potentiate the positive aspects of stress. They can do so through strength of character, self-awareness, fostering interdependence, showing empathy for stress, and drawing on diverse supports.

ANY DISCUSSION OF TEAMS would be incomplete without reviewing the special issues faced by their leaders. Managers may be the most important people to practice raw coping power. If they don't become role models of effective coping, then how should they expect others to deal with work stress?

Managers who walk the talk know about potentiation. Remember, potentiation shows us that we can take on stress as a resource, using its energy to enhance productivity. Healthy managers recognize that how they personally manage stress impacts others. They can succumb to stress or use it to bring out the potential of their team and their entire business. They leverage stressors for the greater good.

Managers can learn to use stress as a team resource through these five pathways. [16]

*Strength of Character:* It may take time and rigorous self-reflection, but managers can adopt virtue-based qualities and a set of ethics that guides their associates to remain strong in the face of stressors. Such virtues include integrity, trust, wisdom, and cooperativeness. They communicate stress as an opportunity for growth. Stress becomes something that can be embraced, build character, and used to help the organization. For example, when a business faces a financial crisis, managers can speak honestly about problems, show compassion, and do their best to embolden the team rather than hide problems, avoid contact, and complain.

*Self-Awareness:* Managers can show an active willingness to self-reflect, stay mindful of their impact on others, and regulate their behavior. They do so by supporting the use of evaluation processes to surface and address issues. For example, with the help of a coach, managers can complete 360 assessments where colleagues anonymously give feedback on leadership skills. Other tools include workshops on conflict management and conducting and responding to employee opinion surveys.

*Socialized Power Motivation:* Managers can cultivate an altruistic motive to positive interpersonal influence, one where they show as much or more concern for the greater good as for their own personal achievement. This motive can over-ride any ego desire to dominate, control, or micro-manage. I have known managers who have demonstrated a desire to channel their power for constructive social ends. This includes taking the time to monitor how stress hurts workers, showing them empathy, and inspiring them to work for the good of the team. I coauthored a book *Heart-Centered Leadership* that guides managers on how to cultivate this motive.

*Requisite Self-Reliance:* Managers should feel secure enough to either use their own stress management skills or to rely on others to help them deal with the often intense and complex work demands that come with leading people. They are interdependent, rather stoically or ruggedly independent. Managers can create a climate that balances self-sufficiency, help-seeking, and help-giving by showing that they don't have to do it all alone, refusing support from others. Instead, they see stressors as opportunities to build strength in the work community. And they draw on the power of community to strengthen each person in their own self-reliance and also encourage them to seek healthy levels of support.

> Who can you go up to right now and sincerely ask, "How can I help?" and put aside your own tensions to transform their stress?

*Diverse Professional Supports:* Healthy managers have good levels of social support, with access to diverse social networks that enhance their quality of work-life. By having diverse supports, not relying only on one group, these managers buffer the negative effects of stress on health. As a result, they frame adverse events, crises, or stressors as factors that can be "taken on" by the workplace community. That is, they cultivate diverse supports not only for their own well-being. Having supportive, multiple, and overlapping networks in any organization helps that organization bounce back from unforeseen adversity. They combine the community and confidence of resilience to create overlapping lines of support throughout their organization. And these diverse supports may be the key to success even in the face of economic downturns. Research suggests that companies that have a culture that values and provides multiple methods of support are more apt to thrive than succumb in the face of harsh challenges.

## The We *in Wellness* [17]

Individual motivation for choosing a higher level of coping may
come only from a shared experience with another or belonging to a
group that has its own positive goals. Being part of the *we* in wellness
may be the necessary trigger for raising our set-point and both
choosing and maintaining a healthy lifestyle.

DR. DEAN ORNISH IS NOTED FOR HIS work on reversing cardiovascular
disease through lifestyle modification, which includes stress management. There is a story that Dr. Ornish and a well-known swami
(Sri Swami Satchidananda) were talking to a group of medical students when someone asked the swami to talk about the difference
between illness and wellness. The swami went to the board at the
front of the room and wrote the words *Illness* and *Wellness*. Then he
circled the *I* in *Illness* and the *We* in *Wellness*. This illustration cap-
tures the importance of the We—compassion, community, having
supports, working together as a team, and avoiding addictive habits.

The *we* in Wellness is truly magical because it is a "force multipli-
er." Only a few people in a group effort may need to practice raw coping power; over time, their behaviors have a ripple effect on others.
This is seen through positive causes to fight disease and participating
in campaigns to raise money, clean the environment, and donate services for health. Other examples include health-related group mem-

berships (such as Weight Watchers, Alcoholics Anonymous, and Biggest Loser campaigns).

This *we* in Wellness can be activated through several pathways:

- Participate in group health activities (examples might be bowling, jogging, cycling, team sports, and dancing).
- Collaborate with others to help the community (such as building a playground for children or picking up litter).
- Join a health-related cause, self-help, or hobby group of any kind (which might be organizing a fun run to raise funds for heart disease or a support group for parents with Down syndrome children).
- Do something to support wellness activities with others at work (join the wellness committee or organize the company health fair).
- Review information on health statistics in your town or county and use this information to build awareness (perhaps your health department conducts health assessments, and the latest report card showed your city had high rates of sexually transmitted infections; work to raise awareness in preventing these infections in your workplace and in community health settings).
- Participate in assessing the work environment and social climate at work in an attempt to raise awareness with others (you might work with a group to select healthier foods for the vending machines or map out a walking path).
- Do an act of random kindness or show support to others.
- Offer to host a potluck for healthy food at work (or ask local truck farmers to bring fresh produce and set up a farmers market in your parking lot).
- Bring in a healthy vegetarian snack that everyone can have at work (instead of a decadent birthday cake).
- Show a movie about healthy lifestyles. Many short videos are available on YouTube about people who changed their lifestyle.

## Summary of the 10 Lenses

1 ▪ *Stressor-Strain:* While stressors can lead to strain and health problems, we can prevent stress from having a negative impact.

2 ▪ *Post-Traumatic Growth:* We can grow from adversity and trauma, learning to both heal and grow from trauma.

3 ▪ *Neuroplasticity:* Our brain is designed for resilience and thriving through inner connections with ourselves and outer connections with community.

4 ▪ *Potentiation:* Stress holds a great potential that we can leverage for the purpose of meaning, growth, and fulfillment.

5 ▪ *Team Resilience:* Five resilience competencies can be cultivated in all individuals and social groups: Centering, Community, Compassion, Confidence, and Commitment.

6 ▪ *Positive Coping Cycle:* We each have an inner guardian—an evaluator—who stands between our stressors and our strain and selects effective coping strategies.

7 ▪ *Negative Coping Cycle:* We can develop ineffective coping habits that place ourselves at risk for addiction.

8 ▪ *Team Awareness:* Our local social connections and the social environment influence our choice between positive and negative coping.

9 ▪ *Manager Pathways for Potentiation:* Leaders can develop, harness, and potentiate the positive stress cycle.

10 ▪ *The We in Wellness:* Being part of the *we* in wellness may be the necessary trigger for raising our set-point and both choosing and maintaining a healthy lifestyle.

A review of these ten models or lenses should bring some optimism, hope, a sense of confidence, and resilience. The research clearly shows, first, that stress does not have to be a problem; and, second, it can actually be a source of strength and growth.

Aside from the negative coping cycle, and its potential for addiction, the other nine models directly indicate solutions for different types of stress. Regarding the negative coping cycle, the tools in this book can be used to prevent, manage, and recover from the poor choices that we make. Many factors can be applied to prevent the negative ravages of stress.

### APPLYING THE LENSES TO OUR RELATIONSHIPS

"People don't care how much you know, unless they also know how much you care." Our knowledge of these models and the basics may be very helpful. And underneath and informing them all is a call to practice these perspectives in our dealings with others. Each of the models speaks directly to the importance of positive community. For example, social support is a primary buffer between stress and strain. Post-traumatic growth is facilitated by contact with helpers—personal and professional—who care about us. Compassion is a key part of resilience, neuroplasticity, and healthy leadership.

Where, then, can we practice these perspectives with others? I have talked a good deal about applying them in the work setting, but the stressors we face in our closest relationships, such as at home, within families, between spouses and partners, among siblings, are critically important to address. Some of us have great jobs and careers and only face real, and sometimes debilitating, strain at home.

Consider this list of some types of interpersonal or family stressors that may require application of positive coping tools:

- Problems with communication: not feeling heard; dealing with a negative, passive-aggressive, or otherwise unhealthy communication pattern

- Inability to resolve conflicts around household routines, chores, cleaning, and other tasks
- Constant arguing
- Facing loss of a loved one through death or disease; dealing with grief and recovery after loss
- Having different beliefs that appear to be irreconcilable
- Dealing with a family member who is in the military and has been deployed or is adjusting after returning from deployment
- Dealing with infidelity or promiscuous behavior in one's partner
- Dealing with a family member who has a problem with addiction
- Raising a child who is unresponsive to discipline or to parental attempts to manage unruly behavior
- Challenges in child-rearing across stages of development (for example, teenage rebellion)
- Difficulty in being able to say no or setting up healthy interpersonal boundaries with in-laws or other relatives
- Carrying a long-term grudge or resentment or interacting with other family members who resist letting go of past harm
- Issues surrounding separation, divorce, and custody
- Having a family that is always involved in some drama, taking sides, or stirring up conflict
- Dealing with infertility or the loss of the ability to bear children
- Coping with financial stress due to conflict around household budget
- Responding to loss of income due to one or more family member's not having a job (lay off, firing, furlough)
- Dealing with aging parents or significant health issues among elderly family members

Clearly, many stressors affect us at home and in our families. Based on just this list, it is obvious that the entire family—as a system—can be vulnerable to stress and trauma. Accordingly, all the tools we have been discussing for building team awareness, team resilience, and the *we* in wellness can be applied to potentiate and leverage stress for positive outcomes.

> The Latin origin of the word *family* [*famulus*] means *servant*; it later meant general household servants, not specifically parents and children. [How can you be a better family servant?]

Let's review some ways that these tools can work. First, the seven basics can be reframed for application to our families, marriages, and love partnerships as follows:

1.  Stressors in our closest family relationships have the potential to provide us with the opportunity for growth and transformation.
2.  Those negative experiences and baggage we feel we received from our upbringing or childhood can be transformed from being the kiss of death to the spice of life.
3.  Regardless of our past, we each have an innate or in-born raw coping power; we can work with marital or family-related stress (past or present) as part of our own transformation.
4.  Our family and upbringing gave us values that, in part, determine the level through which we process stress. We can decide to inherit, adopt, or abandon those values based on whether they help us raise our set-point.
5.  Our relatives, love partnerships, and marriages can help our family members tap into their raw coping power, and together we can transform stress into an experience of thriving at the couple or family level.

6. Families and couples can even go beyond resilience and show audacity in their quest for conversion, peak experiences, flourishing, or thriving.

7. Even when we are under significant family or marital stress, our nervous system is a well-oiled feedback system that allows us to deal with stress at every stage.

Research on marital and family strengthening programs shows that the application of these basic principles can work to help reduce stress and its negative impact.[18] Here are some practical applications of this research:

- Training couples to deal with stressors together can lead to improvements in communication and marital quality. Even just talking with a counselor as a third-party mediator can help iron out issues.

- It is possible to train couples on skills that result in more stable marriages. Financial counseling, for example, can help stabilize a relationship that is threatened by money problems.

- Specific skills can be taught to help family members deal with the stress of having a family member with alcohol or drug addiction.[19] These are available through such tools as a 12-step program (Al-Anon) or a method called CRAFT (Community Reinforcement Approach and Family Training) by Robert J. Meyers, PhD.

- Programs that help family members deal with the stress of caregiving for other family members can be effective. When the burden falls on one person, such as the oldest or only daughter, it's important that other siblings take over some of the care-giving duties, even if it's organizing the finances or hiring outside home care or giving the main caregiver a break.

- General preventive education for marriage and relationships has been shown to produce greater quality in those relationships.

Joining a social or religious group, even a bowling team, can bring quality to stagnant relationships.

For those who are experiencing stress in their relationships, marriages, or families, I hope that these findings also give some hope. The tools presented in the next chapter are designed for general use and may be best applied to workplace or work-oriented situations. However, many of them can be reframed for application to families. For more information on couples and family resources, please consult the Resources section.

# | 3 |

# The 31 Tools for Thriving

CONSIDER THESE STORIES ABOUT financial, relationship, and health resilience before we get into practical applications of the tools in this chapter.[1]

HIS CHILDHOOD WAS MARKED BY POVERTY, domestic violence, alcoholism, sexual abuse, and family illiteracy. Later, this man was separated from his wife and was left to raise his young son while desperately looking for work. Because of his financial situation, he and his son spent their evenings sleeping in homeless shelters, and sometimes restrooms, just to get by. Eventually, the man landed a job and through a very strong work ethic became financially successful. He became so successful that he established his own financial firm. Because of his own transformation, this man now donates time to charities and philanthropy to help others reach their full potential. Twenty years after his days of homelessness the son fondly recalls how much time he got to spend together with his dad.

AFTER SEVERAL YEARS IN A RELATIONSHIP, one man discovered that his fiancée had been having sexual conversations with another man through emails and texting. He immediately confronted her and laid down rules. His fiancée complied by blocking and deleting the other man's phone number and email and gave her fiancé full access to her email account. After some time working on their relationship, this man—like many others who face infidelity—realized that while his trust was fragile it was also strong and resilient.

DOCTORS TOLD A MAN THAT HE HAD A life-threatening illness and, at best, only two to five years left to live. The man at first lost hope, but, through the support of others, he discovered a philosophy that gave him optimism for the future. That philosophy came in the simple words of someone else he knew who was always down on his luck but somehow managed to have faith. Those words were, "It ain't over 'til it's over." Ten years later, this man still lives to tell his story, despite continuing to have the life-threatening illness. He has written books, made and distributed a movie, and seeks to inspire others with his simple message.

What's your story? Yours may not be as dramatic or life trans-forming as these three examples, but your story is about you, and I bet there is some chapter or passage in your story-line that has at least a note of transformation in it. Yes, your story is about YOU, and nobody has a bigger stake in helping you develop your raw coping power than you do.

As you will see, the first tool asks you to tell your resilience story. Or at least to journal about it. Our stories are important, and as we grow and transform, it is also helpful to let go of our stories and not get too caught up in our former identities. And telling your story is a good starting place.

In this chapter you will find an additional thirty different tools that you can use to help strengthen your raw coping power. Some of these tools you may only do once, while others may become a daily habit. Some you may do alone, while others require working with others. Before viewing the tools, this introduction gives you some background so you can get the most out of them.

## BACKGROUND ON THE TOOLS

The different tools provided in this chapter are primarily those my colleagues and I use in our awareness and resilience programs. It is useful, if not essential, to practice each of these more than once and to use a variety to mix it up as the tools reinforce one another. This is why you have a diverse tool-kit. I want you to have a solid sense that you have a rich set of resilience resources at your fingertips.

Research on skill learning suggests several important insights that can help you use the tools to better embody the principles and lenses of raw coping power.

First, it takes initial repetition of a simple manual task to move its procedural content (that would be the steps involved in how to do something) from your short-term to the long-term memory bin.

Second, it takes spaced reminders over time to continue to practice the task so that it becomes more automatic. It is best to practice on a regular basis, even just once a week, than to go long periods without practice.

Third, you must find ways to associate the task with something meaningful in your personal life in order to make the task part of a routine response to situations. Always ask yourself, Why am I doing this? and if you can't connect with a meaningful answer, then find another tool.

Finally, to make a skill a habit, many of us need some reward or reinforcement during the learning process. We need to be rewarded after repeated practice. This reward should come from you. Your own development is your own reward.

There are claims made in the popular training circuit that it takes some specific number of repetitions to establish something as a habit. Some experts say you have to do something fifty times before it becomes a habit. Others say hundreds of times. When it comes to dealing with stress, healthy coping, and resilience, there is no hard and fast rule.

One person could have an immediate one-time radical peak or conversion experience after some major trauma or loss. A wake-up call. As a result, they deeply come to the realization that they need to change their ways. They learn a new skill in a very short time. I know one person who stopped smoking when her boss was diagnosed with lung cancer caused by smoking.

Another person with a long-standing addiction may need long-term treatment with daily exposure to healthy cues and rewards for healthy behaviors. Some people struggle with alcohol their entire lives, but they never stop trying.

I taught learning skills to college students and found that the best learning techniques were those involving preview and preparation, note-taking (highlighting), periodic review, and thinking through the reasons and purpose of the task as it applied to their lives.[2] While all these are great, they are most useful when done with others.

Many of the tools provided here can be used in that way. It is not just the content of each tool that matters but the work you do before and after and how you connect the tools to each other, to your goals, and to your inner guardian.

## THE TOOLS OVERLAP AND REINFORCE ONE ANOTHER

The tools may seem to be repetitive. Over the years in working with people and in my own life, I have found that we stop using a tool after single or short-term use either because it gets old, becomes a mindless routine, or we just don't like it. Or, more fundamentally, you just keep taking the path of least resistance. As Robert Fritz suggests in his book *The Path of Least Resistance*, many of us do not look at the fundamental and entrenched structures of our lives and find lasting and creative ways to make changes.

But it may not be so fundamental. You may just need a nudge. Some people are more drawn to one tool versus another due to some slight difference that makes one more attractive. For this reason, I encourage you to find those exercises you like and repeat them every once in a while (once a week, twice a month) and then return and try others. Think of the tools as little self-nudges.

You may find yourself using one tool and think it is too similar to another tool. But there is a simple reason that these tools overlap. We have to lay happy grooves down in our brain and reinforce those grooves with nearby friends and lovers. Let's give a simple example.

Let's say you cognitively understand and tell yourself one main idea in this book, namely, "I can prevent stress from having a negative impact on my life." You can tell yourself that one phrase over and over until you really believe it to be true, and this may work. Unfortunately, simple repetition of a single phrase will not "take" if there are other factors in the way. This includes other conflicting beliefs, memory, attitude, personality, or an environment that tells you, usually in an unconscious way, I have so many problems that it can't be true that I can transform stress.

Because you realize it takes more than just repeating a phrase, you turn to a tool in this book. You realize that you have to "work it" to embody the principle in a deeper way. And you use a tool. Let's say

Tool #7: Knowing Your Early Warning Signs, and you discover that the first thing you have to do is pay more attention to how stress impacts your body.

Later on, you use Tool #17: "Reviewing your coping style factors" and realize that your lifestyle is preventing you from paying attention to these stress signals. Then, you go back and use Tool #6: "Values exercise: Setting the set-point," and it dawns on you that one of the reasons that you have not been healthy enough is because you have not taken the time to focus on what matters most in your life or those real abiding values that you believe are important to a life well lived.

This simple example is not meant to show you that you should have started with Tool #6 on values. Rather, it is meant to encourage you to explore the tools in a way that works for you and to find the connections yourself. It is always better when you have your own self-generated insights. I want you to enjoy discovering your raw coping power on your own and as a result of your own intuitive exploration.

Every tool relates to every other tool in some way. One person may have an insight by doing Tool #28" "Work-Life Borders" that leads him or her to go back and re-do another tool in a new way and have a momentous new understanding that would never have happened before.

## Doing the Tools In or Out of Sequence

This takes us to a commonly asked question: *Should I do the tools in order, beginning with number 1 and then number 2, and so on?* I encourage you to do whatever works. There is no single, correct approach. As I hoped the previous example showed, it is better for you to find your own way. At the same time, some raw coping power champions may enjoy this general order or framework.

*Foundational Tools:* Tools #1 through #6 help to lay a basic foundation because it is important to know your own story of resilience, take an inventory of current stressors, and explore your current set-point for happiness and for thriving from stress. It is also critical to adapt a daily mind-body practice and establish a meaningful reason for doing this work. A later exercise, Tool #14, reminds you of the importance of your set-point and helps you review it more deeply.

*Inner Guardian Work:* Tools #7 through #13 take you through a sequence of exercises to help you strengthen your evaluation and observation skills or your inner guardian. This includes not only recognizing your stress warning signs but also recognizing how you tolerate stress and deciding what actions you may need to take should you be too tolerant (or intolerant) of problems. You also have to protect your inner guardian and sometimes that means seeking help and support from others, including professionals.

*Embody Stress > Evaluate > Cope:* Tools #15 through #21 may actually be done in sequence and as a way to create a set of meaningful intentions or goals that you can use as daily thrive-reminders. The S>E>C model or positive coping cycle really surrounds your inner guardian and helps you transform stress into opportunities to thrive. These tools provide a specific sequence for supporting that process. A later exercise, Tool #29, reinforces the model through a visualization exercise.

*Uplifts!:* Tools #22 and #23 re-introduce the importance of focusing on the positive. Recall that Principle #6 suggests that there are many more positive aspects to life than negative, and you can use the energy provided by positivity to go beyond resilience and show audacity. These two exercises help you see the positive uplifts in your life.

*Integrative Exercises:* There are two tools that integrate or synthesize previous tools. Tool #24 involves bringing together those other previous exercises. This is a more in-depth exercise than most of the others in the book and helps you integrate your learning. Tool #29 reinforces the Positive Coping Cycle.

*Positive Framing Tools:* The other tools provide additional insights and, while each stands alone, they all have one thing in common. They are designed to help you get in touch with the most positive, uplifting, and potentiating aspects of yourself. This includes areas such as work (the job crafting tool), work-life balance, your resilience qualities (the Five Cs tool), and relationships (the Really Listening tool).

## PREPARING FOR TOOL USE: IDENTIFYING STRESS DOMAINS

Isn't it unfortunate that crisis is the best way to make stress management a relevant topic? Relevance is everything.

Many people don't seek help until they are faced with a crisis. So it is worth taking the time to ask yourself these three questions to prepare for tool use. I want you to make sure that your time and effort is relevant!

- In what domains of my life am I experiencing the most stress (relationships, work and career, health, finances, or something else)?
- In what domains do I feel the least prepared or the most vulnerable when there is stress?
- In what domains do I tend to experience the same problems over and over again?

Answering these questions will help you get focused when you use any of the tools. To further help with identifying stress domains, take a look at these lists. Check off any item that is relevant to you right now.

| Relationships | | Work and Career | |
|---|---|---|---|
| ○ | Parenting stress | ○ | Out of work or career derailment |
| ○ | Family responsibilities | | |
| ○ | Arguments, disagreements, conflicts | ○ | Not adequately rewarded |
| | | ○ | Poor or inadequate benefits |
| ○ | Separation, estrangement, divorce | ○ | Politics in the office |
| | | ○ | Bullying or discrimination |
| ○ | Grudges or unresolved issues | ○ | Burnout, job insecurity |
| ○ | Jealousy and envy | ○ | Favoritism or nepotism |
| ○ | Loneliness or social isolation | ○ | Unreasonable demands/deadlines |
| ○ | Bullying or discrimination | | |
| ○ | Feeling excluded, not belonging | ○ | Micromanagement |
| ○ | Anxiety around people | ○ | Mergers and acquisitions |
| ○ | Anger or irritation with others | ○ | Too much commuting |
| ○ | Petty issues, rumors, gossip | ○ | Not enough independence |
| Health | | Financial | |
| ○ | Lack of energy or sleep problems | ○ | Rising costs (food, gas, other) |
| | | ○ | Insurance problems |
| ○ | Mood problems (anxiety, sadness) | ○ | Living paycheck to paycheck |
| | | ○ | Loans and debts |
| ○ | Other mental health issues | ○ | Credit card problems |
| ○ | Recovering from illness | ○ | Loss or downgrade of income |
| ○ | Chronic disease | ○ | Exposed to theft or robbery |
| ○ | Loss or deterioration of function | ○ | Budget mismanagement |
| ○ | Unable to control weight | ○ | Disagreements about money |
| ○ | Respiratory problems | ○ | Failure to adequately plan |
| ○ | Skin problems | ○ | Retirement concerns |
| ○ | Cardiovascular issues | ○ | Gambling problems |
| ○ | Digestive or intestinal problems | | |
| ○ | Surgery | | |

Every now and then, come back to this list. You may notice that the items you checked now are no longer a concern in the future. Generally, your list will get shorter if you actively work the tools in this chapter. I say "generally" because in some special circumstances you may need additional support that the tools may not provide.

## Marry Domain Skills with Raw Coping Power

Several tools in this chapter deal directly with knowing your limits and knowing when it is time to seek professional help. It also helps to recognize that within each of the four domains (relationships, work and career, health, and financial) you may require additional and special skills designed to help you solve problems that are unique to that domain. Let's briefly review some underlying reasons for problems in each domain and then the types of resources or skills you may need.

One point of this review is to show that even if you do an excellent job of transforming your stress, it is still possible that an additional set of skills may be helpful. Another point is that even if you have these domain-specific skills, you will be more effective with them when you are also tapping into your raw coping power. Let's consider ...

Some, if not most, of your relationship stress may be due to any of the following: poor communication and listening skills, low emotional intelligence, poor perspective-taking, unresolved issues from the past, failure to take necessary time with each other, some type of relationship addiction, complexity in the relationship (a step family is a prime example), physical distance, lack of mutual problem solving skills, and more.

Some, if not most, of your work/career stress may be due to larger problems in the economy, problems in marketing, poor training, poor management, failures to communicate needs or be actively heard around those needs, managerial problems that are caused by a lack of training, lack of vision, lack of teamwork, poorly defined policies, lack of accountability, unhelpful role models, and more.

Some, if not most, of your health stress may be due to typical failures to incorporate a healthy lifestyle (diet, exercise, rest, sleep), not knowing enough about your nutritional and dietary needs, ignoring underlying factors associated with the problem, exposure to certain environmental toxins, genetic risks, or an addiction to unhealthy foods and substances (sugar, alcohol, fatty foods).

Some, if not most, of your financial stress may be due to lack of skills in any of these areas: budget management, unwise spending on entertainment or other diversions, large purchases, debt mismanagement, lack of an emergency fund, not discussing money with spouse or partner, failure to understand employee benefits, failure to diversify investments, and plenty more money problems.

It should be obvious that in every one of these domains just having stress management skills may not be sufficient. There are a wealth of books, tapes, programs, professionals, counselors, and other tools that can help. I suggest marrying those tools with domain-specific skills and resources as follows:

For relationship stress, consider taking the time to share your personal resilience story (Tool #1), and your personal learning about raw coping power (#21), and do the Paired Uplift (#23) and Really Listening exercise (#30). For skills, read a book or take a course on communication.[3] This includes Elizabeth Kuhnke's Communication Skills for Dummies or Marshall Rosenberg's books, tapes, or workshops on Nonviolent Communication (see www.cnvc.org), or a workshop from Dale Carnegie Training (see www.dalecarnegie.com). There are also books and workshops on emotional intelligence (for research see http://ei.yale.edu).[4] If your marriage is having serious problems, consider a marriage and family therapist (find one at the Association of Marriage and Family Therapists or www.aamft.org).

For work or career stress, consider reviewing the lenses on Team Awareness (Lens #8), Five Cs of Resilience (#9), and Manager Potentiation (#10). See if your workplace will purchase copies of Raw Coping Power for your coworkers or team and distribute and have a discussion about these ideas. Then consider distributing the job crafting tool (#25) and asking colleagues to discuss their plans. You can also do a review of the Five Cs together (Tool # 25).

Of course, to address job stress you may also need to sharpen your skills and get more training (see the American Society for Training and Development, www.astd.org). For serious problems with harassment, bullying, or discrimination, then it is also important to contact your human resources department (see Society for Human Resources, www.shrm.org).

Many workplaces have an employee assistance program (EAP) that provides counseling and other resources to employees and family members at no cost (see www.eapassn.org or www.easna.org). Finally, an Appendix at the end of this book provides a few corporate or organizational tools that may be useful to job stress consultants or those in human resources and organizational development.

For health stress, the most important tool you can use is Tool #2, adapting a daily mind-body practice. I highly recommend the set of tools (#15 to #21) to embody Stress > Evaluate > Cope. There are two general health skill categories: preventive and reparative. For prevention, it may help to find a personal health trainer, join a gym, schedule a massage (regularly!), participate in a weight loss group, or use any of the online wellness programs or smartphone applications designed to address a particular need. For repair, consider visiting a medical doctor, chiropractor, naturopath, or a specialist for advice. You may also go on a health retreat, a fasting diet (with proper supervision), or consider an herbal or homeopathic remedy.

For financial stress, it is possible that any set of tools can be helpful, depending on your situation. However, like work stress, many problems may be due to the economy and factors that are beyond your control. So it is important to put financial stress in perspective. Look at any tool and revise the tool to apply more to money and finances. For example, the Four Questions (Tool #5) ask about health, but you can revise these to pertain to money. Keep in mind that being financially healthy is not the same thing as having a lot of money. In fact, many rich people are not healthy because they worry about finances or have lost control over spending.

- Am I financially healthy (living comfortably within my means, successful, abundant)?
- How do I really know if I am financially healthy?
- Could I be financially healthier?
- What would it take?

Many tools and resources are available to help with financial stress, including books on budgeting and budget calculators you can find online or through a local bank. Seek agencies and resources, including Consumer Credit Counseling (www.consumercredit.com), consumer advisory resources such as Clark Howard (www.clarkhoward.com), Consumer Reports (www.consumerreports.org), or Suze Orman (www.suzeorman.com). Other great resources are financial advisors (see www.napfa.org) or financial planners (see www.fpanet.org).

## STORIES AND MOVIES

Many stories, both fiction and nonfiction, help motivate us to be more resilient, thrive, and flourish. There are several true story examples provided in this book. I encourage you to find those stories that inspire you or that you most resonate with and review them as often as you like. There are also resources for reflecting on movies and tying their messages into your own growth. Please consult the Resources section for using movies to enhance your coping power.

---

IMPORTANT TIP: RIGHT EFFORT, COMPASSION, AND REST

The tools are best approached with an attitude of positive exploration and a sense of ease. If "doing" any tool leads to tension, your mind-body system is sending you a message to move toward "being." That would be funny. A book on stress management that causes you stress! Nonetheless, some exercises may stir up emotions, so go easy.

I encourage participants in my workshops to listen for their own solutions, to experiment with tools, and to also give themselves permission to relax. At a pre-workshop public talk I gave, one woman told me she did not need the workshop: "Dr. Bennett, I wish I knew about this before I retired from years of a very stressful career." I was surprised then that she showed up for a day-long retreat and took most of the day to nap on a couch. She revealed that she had just not given herself the permission to take time out to nourish her own raw coping power.

By now, you hopefully realize that the answer does not lie in the tools but in how you work them. Try this simple formula:

1. *Right Effort.* Pace yourself, keeping in mind that your purpose is to develop good, wholesome, and positive skills. Focus more on what you are nurturing rather than on what you are battling.
2. *Compassion.* Tell yourself that you deserve to have some relief, that you genuinely care about your own well-being.
3. *Rest.* Check in with your need for energy and for both physical and mental rest. Take a 5-minute nap if that is what you need.

## THE LIST OF TOOLS

This table provides a brief overview of each tool with just a hint as to why you might consider using it.

| The Tool | Why use this tool and do the exercise? |
|---|---|
| 1. Telling your Resilience Story | *Know your own strength.* Tap into or remind yourself (and others) that your life has some solid proof of raw coping power. |
| 2. Adapting a Daily Mind-Body Practice | *Build your personal reserves.* Create the conditions to readily access your higher coping ability at any time. |
| 3. Listing Stressors and Ways of Coping | *Recognize your inner guardian.* It helps to inventory your current stress-response situation WITH your guardian in mind. |
| 4. Tapping into Your Willingness and Set-Point | *Expand your willingness.* Taking a close look at your level may inspire you to raise your sights even higher. |
| 5. The Four Questions | *Be really and truly healthy.* You should have your own internal sense of what it means to be really healthy. |
| 6. Values Exercise: Setting the Set-Point | *Know where you are headed.* Very often your values determine what you are willing to settle for, stand for, and go for. |
| 7. Knowing Your Early Warning Signs (strain signature) | *Be mindful of stress impact.* You have a unique way that stress shows up in your mind-body being. It helps to tune in. |

| | The Tool | Why use this tool and do the exercise? |
|---|---|---|
| 8. | Breathing into and through Your Strain | *Tune in further and let go.* This follows from and deepens the previous exercise. |
| 9. | Knowing Your Tolerance Levels for Strain | *Respect your inner "tolerator."* Do you need to take action in an area that has become unworkable and let go in other areas that are workable? Which ones? |
| 10. | Developing a Flexible Window for Tolerance | *Be even more open to resilience.* This systematic exercise challenges you to find healthy responses instead of tolerating. |
| 11. | Knowing Your Limits of Strain and Tolerance | *Respond in ways that improve the situation.* This deepens the prior exercise: reflect on positive response choices you do have. |
| 12. | Preventive Help-Seeking | *Don't ignore available help.* Even with the tools you have, know what types of help are available so you can choose to use them. |
| 13. | Knowing Your Later Warning Signs | *Know when it is time to get help.* Those people who thrive in life also know the signs that say it is time to get help. |
| 14. | Set-Point Review | *Keep learning and growing.* This inventory tool may help you take it to the next level ... past coping, past resilience, to thriving! |
| 15. | Adapting the Stress > Evaluate > Cope Framework | *Welcome your inner guardian.* On any given day, you can welcome an inner resource that knows how to cope effectively. |

| The Tool | Why use this tool and do the exercise? |
|---|---|
| 16. Reviewing Your Healthy Lifestyle Factors | *Know your specific lifestyle strengths.* This survey will help you focus on areas you need to strengthen for even higher function. |
| 17. Reviewing Your Coping Style Factors | *Know your specific coping strength.* Review the many ways you cope and think about letting go of the ineffective habits. |
| 18. Celebrating Strengths and Choosing a New Goal | *Celebrate new strengths you want.* Reawaken your desire for fulfillment by setting your sights on new areas of growth. |
| 19. Goal Setting and Positive Intentions Exercise | *Take the time to craft your intention well.* This exercise helps you focus on a specific stressor with steps to transform it. |
| 20. Mind-Body Infusing of Your Intention | *Infuse your intention into your mind-body system.* This follows from and deepens the previous exercise. |
| 21. Follow-up: Sharing, Reminders, Relapse Prevention | *Keep following up with yourself.* Just doing these tools once will not work unless you follow up. This exercise helps. |
| 22. Focus on the Positive: Generating Uplifts | *Focus on the positive.* If you think your life is just a downer, you may be looking in the wrong places. Check this out. |
| 23. Paired Uplift Exercise | *Focus on the positive with others.* Two heads are better than one? This exercise says "two happy hearts are better than one." |

| The Tool | Why use this tool and do the exercise? |
|---|---|
| 24. Visualization: Future Self for Efficacy, Hope, Optimism | *Take the time to integrate your learning.* Do this exercise only if you are ready to really create a powerful raw coping engine. |
| 25. Job Crafting | *Don't let your job run your life.* There are ways to look on the bright side. They may be small but they are systematic and effective. |
| 26. Five Cs of Resilience | *Find your own way to resonate with resilience.* It could be your mind, your body, your emotions. This exercise gives you options. |
| 27. Thrive Mapping | *Create your future self as a real thriver.* Mapping out how you respond to stress in the future can make it so. |
| 28. Work-Life Borders | *Find empty spaces in your life to just hang out.* In the brief time you are on the planet, it helps to contemplate and deepen yourself. |
| 29. Visualization: Building Your Centering Protective Shield | *Nurture your inner guardian.* This grand exercise helps you realize that you may be protected in ways you had not realized. |
| 30. Managing Stressful Communication: Really Listening | *Play nice and listen.* This entire program is not a "go it alone" deal. To receive you have to give and this does it. |
| 31. NUDGING Self | *Small steps.* A "saving the best for last" exercise. So think about starting here, stopping here along the way, and ending here. |

## A Guarantee

If we had the full strength of consciousness to pay undivided attention, we would realize in a glaring "light of day" manner that what we label as stress is actually the very thing we need to gain more mastery of our life. In our self-remembering state and with even an inkling of this possible attitude toward stress, we would be more inclined to be bold and audacious in our ways of approaching problems rather than avoiding or shrinking from those keen challenges that await us.

But is it true that we lack this full strength of consciousness because we allow ourselves to be distracted by society and technology? Do we sacrifice our essential raw coping power for the beguiling comforts, conveniences, and novelty of an ever-growing number of devices? Consider just the latest electronic gadgets, pieces of software, or smartphone applications. We habitually turn our attention toward these novelties often to divert our precious energy from the real inner work required to cultivate and refine our original and essential power to thrive and flourish.

To gain the most from this tool section, you have to bring the full strength of your consciousness. You have to have the intention. Imagine that you are being called to do the serious work of cultivating and refining that inner sense. Every idea and tool is provided with the intention of awakening you to this calling: activating your inner guardian, expanding your zone of tolerance, traversing your "thrive map," potentiating your life, embracing your own neuroplasticity, developing each of the Five Cs of resilience, and nudging yourself.

Before using a tool, sit alone in a room and remove all distractions. Bring your full will to the task with earnestness. Pay attention and contact your wakeful self.

I guarantee that if you are steadfast in this attitude, you will never experience what you currently call "stress" again.

## TOOL #1
## Telling Your Resilience Story

*Purpose:* To reinforce your identity as a person who not only copes with, but also thrives from, stress and to continue to learn about your personal resilience journey by yourself or with and through others.

*Description:* You can do this alone as a journal exercise with the facilitated questions. Just go directly to Step 2 below. You can also prepare a time where you gather with others to share. To create a sense of safety and intimacy, a general rule is to allow about ten to fifteen minutes a person in a group of four to eight people. This meeting can occur in a variety of settings: after a shared meal, on a spiritual retreat, or as part of a broader stress management workshop. Here are some general guidelines for announcing and facilitating the meeting.

---

### TELLING YOUR RESILIENCE STORY (ANNOUNCEMENT)

Every person has challenges that shape their character, help them grow, and make them stronger. What challenges have you faced that helped you define your inner strength? Join us to share and learn from each other in the spirit of growth.

#### Our Resilience Stories (Guidelines & Questions)

Each group requires a facilitator whose role is to announce the CHAT guidelines, ensure everyone agrees and abides by them, monitor participant time, and model active listening.

*Step 1.* Read the guidelines and ask everyone to raise their hand or say yes in agreement:

(C) Confidentiality: What's said here stays here; (H) Honor: Give your full respect and attention when it is others' time to speak; (A) Anonymity: Avoid using the names of other people in your own story to show respect for them; (T) Trust: Make sure everyone gets an opportunity by honoring time limits.

*Step 2.* Read the following questions: The following questions work in different ways for different people. Feel free to answer any one or all as you feel comfortable. (1) Is there a story of resilience that inspires you? (2) What challenges have made you stronger? Why? What strength do you now have as a result? (3) How have you continued to, or how will you, cultivate this strength by creating or facing new challenges?

*Note.* When doing this exercise with others: After each person finishes, take a minute to have one or two people in the group share their gratitude and point out the positive strengths revealed in the story.

JOURNALING

If you have never written in a journal before, you can use *Raw Coping Power* to get started. You can enhance the exercises in this section by writing your responses in your own personal and private journal and watch your growth over time.

Keeping a journal is a positive way to chart your own course of self-discovery with a purpose or goal. Your goal can be raising your set-point, transforming stress, facing and overcoming a particular challenge, starting a new chapter in your life, or simply navigating and exploring the tools in this chapter. Some readers also prefer to write their responses on a separate page and not write in this book. To get started simply purchase a blank, bound book and favorite special pen.

TOOL #2

Adapting a Daily Mind-Body Practice

*Purpose:* To develop positive routines and habits that activate the body's natural healing properties (The Healer Within).

*Description:* A variety of practices can be done for ten to sixty minutes or longer as part of your daily routine, just like bathing, diet, exercise, work, rest, and sleep. Such practices include meditation, repetition of a positive phrase, biofeedback, guided visualizations, relaxation techniques, journaling, Tai Chi, Qigong, other movement therapies (such as Feldenkrais, Alexander Technique), Pilates, yoga, silent prayer, and energy work. Choose a method that works for you and be open to explore options.

*Example:* Several visualization examples are provided in this section. One mind-body technique is called "autogenic training" developed by Johannes Heinrich Schultz in 1932. This technique involves repeating a set of visualizations in fifteen-minute sessions at different times of the day (for example, morning, lunch, and evening).

The script for one version of an autogenic technique is in the box. This script would be read aloud slowly, sometimes with soothing background music, or tape-recorded and replayed while you are sitting or lying down. Do not practice just before or while operating heavy machinery or driving.

---

*Relaxation Script (read in calming and slow pace)*

Read each phrase, pause for five to ten seconds, and repeat the same phrase before going to the next:
- My arms and legs are heavy and warm.
- My heartbeat is calm and regular.
- My breathing is free and easy.
- My abdomen is warm.
- My forehead is cool.
- My mind is quiet and still.

---

This technique and all others presented in this book should not be considered as medical advice. If you are concerned about ongoing stress, severe stress, or trauma, please seek professional help from a medical doctor or licensed psychologist.

TOOL #3
Listing Stressors and Ways of Coping

*Purpose:* To enhance a sense of your inner guardian by developing a framework and intention for the positive coping cycle:

Stress ➜ Evaluate ➜ Cope

*Exercise:* Using the following five-step exercise, you begin as follows:

❶ Write down a list of five to ten current stressors from personal or home life and work, including any self-generated or internal stressors.

❷ Next to this list, write down five to ten ways you cope with these stressors. Next, use the framework and sequence that follows (❸ ❹ ❺). Contemplate what can "take a stand" between the Stressors and the Ways you Cope. Get in touch with your inner guardian: whatever it is that lets you slow down, pause, and reflect.

| ❶ List Stressors | Evaluate | ❷ List Ways You Cope |
|---|---|---|
| ○ | ❹ Describe Your Inner Guardian | ○ |
| ○ | | ○ |
| ○ | | ○ |
| ○ | | ○ |
| ○ | | ❸ Circle effective ways in above list |

❸ Review your list of ways you cope in column 2 and circle all those ways that are healthy, helpful, or effective in dealing with the stressors. Review again and underline or place an X next to those that are unhealthy or ineffective.

❹ Reflect on what happens "in between" the Stressors and your EFFECTIVE coping habits. What is it about you (inner resources, strengths, values, attitudes) that leads you to be a positive coping machine? Remember, this is a positive aspect of your inner guardian. Write down all those positive qualities you associate with your inner guardian.

❺ Craft a positive statement about your inner guardian based on your notes in step 4. Write that down on a separate index card or Post-it note and tape it to your mirror or on something you look at regularly as a reminder. Use any of the terms in the following box or design your own:

---

My positive intention begins with:

"My guardian is" or "I am" or "I know how"

Then add (as you see fit): strong ● clear ● relaxed ● mindful ● compassionate ● ready to greet challenge ● open to new experiences ● sees the gift when I stumble ● ready to move on ● able to let go ● open to the challenge ● acts with integrity ● *or any other word or phrase that you like.*

Remember to play with this statement until it fits you.

---

Tool #4

Tapping into Your Willingness and Set-Point

*Purpose:* To embrace rather than succumb to stress by reflecting on your motivation, willingness, and energy to set higher aspirations for positive experiences (such as optimism, hope, and resilience).

*Exercise:* Using the diagram/survey on the next page, this three-step exercise helps you gauge your willingness to expand your set-point.

❶ Indicate how much you agree with the "My Willingness" statement, using the 0 to 100 scale. Write that number down. In this work—your raw coping power—a single point change, whether it is from 9 to 10 or 98 to 99 can be a "tipping point" or dramatic shift.

❷ Review the seven statements in the "My Level" area and check the statement (or check in between two statements) that describes your current experience. Note that your willingness may feel higher or lower than your level. You may be more willing to expand your capacity than your current level would suggest. Conversely, your willingness may be lower than your level. Either of these is fine.

❸ Now, reflecting on your two ratings (My Willingness and My Level), ask yourself two questions:

- Am I where I need to be in my life? and
- What motivates me to expand my level (examples might be health, family, productivity, success, spirituality)?

Journal your answer to these two questions.

## My Willingness

I am willing to expand
my current capacity
for enhanced
happiness, health,
success,
abundance, or
productivity

Strongly Agree   100

90

80

Agree

70

60

In Between   50

40

30

Disagree

20

10

Strongly Disagree   0

## My Level

I remain excited about life every day; regardless of what positive or negative events occur I always learn and grow.

I am happy today with all the situations of my life; I am able to bounce back from negative events and keep going strong.

I am now coping with stress in healthy ways (such as exercise, problem solving, meeting stress head on, positive self-talk) and will continue to do so.

I am just getting by right now with life's ups and downs.

I seem to often cope with stress in unhealthy ways (such as unhealthy eating, zoning out, negative self-talk, avoiding issues).

I have an unhealthy habit or addiction that keeps me from full functioning, happiness and health.

I remain depressed or distressed by life's negative events or stressors; I am not sure I can deal with it all.*

*If your level is very low consider the US National Suicide Prevention hotline 1 (800) 273-8255

TOOL #5

The Four Questions

*Purpose:* To develop a refined sense of your set-point and identify three influences on that set-point: your personal attitudes and motivations, the work environment, and the home (friends and family) environment.

*Exercise:* Asking specific questions of yourself and taking the time to reflect on the answers can help you develop an inner sense of self-knowledge.

❶ Review these questions, applying them to personal health.

    1.   Am I healthy? (LEVEL; refer to levels in Tool #4)
    2.   How do I really know if I am healthy? (MONITOR)*
    3.   Could I be healthier? (MAKEOVER)
    4.   What would it take? (DO IT!)

Journal answers to these questions. Be honest with yourself.

❷ Review these same questions, applying to your work.

    1.   Is my workplace healthy (leaders, coworkers, financially, ethically)?
    2.   How do I really know if it is healthy?*
    3.   Could it be healthier?
    4.   What would it take?

Again, journal your answers. Are they the same or different from ❶?

❸ Review the questions, applying to family and friends.

    1.   Is my family healthy (the whole family system, best friends)?
    2.   How do I really know if it is healthy?*
    3.   Could it be healthier?
    4.   What would it take?

Again, journal your answers. Notice if they differ from ❶ or ❷.

❹ There is no right or wrong answer to these questions. Many people answer Q1 (LEVEL) and Q3 (MAKEOVER) with "It depends; sometimes the answer is yes and sometimes no. So it's hard to give a straight answer." Others answer Q2 (MONITOR) and Q4 (DO IT!) with "I am not sure."

In this next step, just notice if you either (A) tend toward "It depends" or a "not sure" attitude, or (B) have a clear sense of the answer that keeps you vigilant to your current level and energized around your willingness. It is your responsibility to be mindful of what you are either *standing* for or *settling* for. Do you stay on top of your self-care or do you let it slack? Do you binge (indulge in unhealthy habits) and then purge (restrict your compulsiveness too much)?

The key is to understand which areas of your life raise your set-point to higher levels: you, your workplace, and/or your family. Whatever it is, hold on to those forces that keep you healthy, keep you monitoring your health, and keep you moving up!

*Note on Monitoring.* You may ask yourself how you can monitor your health and that of your workplace and family. Start with your personal health by getting your annual check-up. This includes your weight, body mass index, waist circumference, blood pressure, and cholesterol levels. Everyone in your family should do the same.

If there are any risks, your doctor may advise you to monitor more regularly on your own. You can also encourage your coworkers to get checkups. If you don't have a worksite wellness program, talk to your boss or human resource director. Most of these programs include some type of personal health assessment.

There are also survey tools that measure the health of the climate in your family and workplace. Contact the author or visit our website to learn more: www.organizationalwellness.com.

TOOL #6
Values Exercise: Setting the Set-Point

*Purpose:* To discern which values may be driving your willingness, your set-point, and your experience of Principle #4 at work in your life: *My values help shape and determine my set-point.*

*Background:* We tend to want to live in ways that fulfill our values. Look over the grid of values below. These give life meaning and give us a sense of direction in life. Different people have different values, and values can change over time. Values are important because they drive our self-care behaviors, how we handle stress, and our happiness set-point. For example, one person may take better care of herself because she values family and parenting; she wants to be present and function well so she can be with her loved ones. Another person might take care of himself because he values his career and employment and wants to stay healthy to handle the stress of the job.

*Exercise.* From the following list, select the **top three values** that motivate you to stay mindful of stress. Why are you interested in mastering stress? For what value? (Note: Consider sharing your response with a close friend, loved one, or spouse and then do the same for them.)

Grid of Values

| Family | Being a Couple (Marriage/Intimacy) | Parenting |
|---|---|---|
| Security | Beauty | Spirituality |
| Physical Health | Career or Employment | Citizenship or Community |
| Education or Personal Growth | Recreation or Hobby or Sport | Friendship |
| Enjoyment | Achievement | Wealth |
| Conformity | Maturity | Self-Direction |
| A Life of Integrity | Leaving a Legacy | Helping Humanity |

## Tool #7
### Knowing Your Early Warning Signs (strain signature)

*Purpose:* To train yourself to monitor signals that indicate you are under initial strain and to respond to those signals in healthy ways.

*Background:* Each of us has our own "strain signature" or our unique way of starting to sense that (1) we are not responding well to stress and (2) we may need to do a course correction.

*Exercise:* Reflect on the most recent times you experienced strain. From each of the following images and lists, check items that are the common signs you experience in any or all of the four areas: physical, emotional, cognitive, or social. Ask yourself three questions:

- How long does it take me before I begin to recognize the sign(s)?
- What prevents me from recognizing the sign(s)?
- What healthy habits help me recognize and address the sign(s)?

Consider whether you tend to notice early signs only when work suffers. For example, do you pay more attention to work than to your body? Do you notice decreases in job involvement, conscientiousness, or cooperation; or when you start to feel burned-out? If so, ask the three questions again and explore if one of the signs happens first.

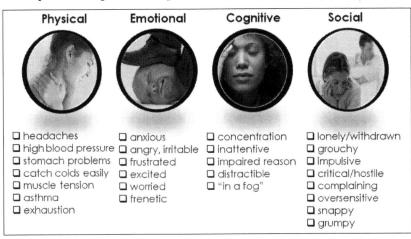

| Physical | Emotional | Cognitive | Social |
|---|---|---|---|
| ❑ headaches | ❑ anxious | ❑ concentration | ❑ lonely/withdrawn |
| ❑ high blood pressure | ❑ angry, irritable | ❑ inattentive | ❑ grouchy |
| ❑ stomach problems | ❑ frustrated | ❑ impaired reason | ❑ impulsive |
| ❑ catch colds easily | ❑ excited | ❑ distractible | ❑ critical/hostile |
| ❑ muscle tension | ❑ worried | ❑ "in a fog" | ❑ complaining |
| ❑ asthma | ❑ frenetic | | ❑ oversensitive |
| ❑ exhaustion | | | ❑ snappy |
| | | | ❑ grumpy |

TOOL #8

Breathing Into and Through Your Strain

*Purpose:* To tune in to your mind-body wisdom and recognize Principle #7 at work in your life: *My nervous system is a well-oiled feedback system, allowing me to deal with stress at every stage.*

*Background:* This exercise can activate a "relaxation response," a term coined by Dr. Herbert Benson to indicate your ability to release chemicals and brain signals that make your muscles and organs slow down, increasing blood flow to the brain.

*Exercise:* Follow the steps to cultivate a growing internal sense of calmness, nurturing, and spaciousness. Breathe calmly and deeply.

❶ *Drink a glass of water.* Review your strain signature information from Tool #7, "Knowing Your Early Warning Signs." Select your top three signs (no more than three) that are your earliest or most reliable signals, like mindful sentries who surround your inner resilience guardian, on the lookout for possible danger.

❷ *One at a time, create a feeling or sensation of space or spaciousness that surrounds each sign as follows:*

- Close your eyes.
- Begin with deep breathing. Consider using the Relaxation Script from Tool #2.
- Bring loving attention to each sign. For physical sensations, bring attention to that area of your body. For emotional or mental states, gently re-create the mental state. For social reactions, recall a time you acted that way, attending to sensations and feelings.
- Taking one minute per sign, repeat internally, This [name the sensation] is floating in space, relaxation surrounds it, spaciousness, allowing.

❸ *Allow your signature to just be there.* Just be with and breathe into it. Recognize internally that your signature is a healthy feedback system. Thank it for being there by repeating to yourself: *I am giving you some time off today because you do such a great job. My early warning signs keep me relaxed. I know they work when I need them. I can give them a much deserved chance to rest.*

## TOOL #9
### Knowing Your Tolerance Levels for Strain

*Purpose:* To honor your feedback system that chooses how much strain is tolerable; build respect for your sense of healthy tolerance.

*Background:* Each of us varies in how much we put up with, suffer through, allow, stomach, or tolerate pain, stressors, and strains in our lives, whether these are external, self-created, or self-imposed. We can develop a long-term habit of tolerating such problems, and we always have the ability to change that habit and tolerance level. Our tolerance is an important part of our happiness set-point.

*Exercise:* Complete this five-item survey. Sum up scores to arrive at a total between 6 (low) and 30 (high). Review your scores, and ask yourself if you have healthy tolerance (not too high or too low).

| | | | | | |
|---|---|---|---|---|---|
| 1. Does your tolerance for stress lead to physical or mental problems? | Not at all ① | A little ② | Some ③ | Much ④ | Greatly ⑤ |
| 2. Most situations at work are difficult to tolerate. | Never ① | A little ② | Some ③ | Mostly ④ | Always ⑤ |
| 3. Most situations at home are difficult to tolerate. | Never ① | A little ② | Some ③ | Mostly ④ | Always ⑤ |
| 4. Is your tolerance for stress better on certain days during the week? | My tolerance is better at certain times ① | | In between ③ | | I have difficulty tolerating stress every day ⑤ |
| 5. Is your tolerance for stress better at certain times of the year? | My tolerance is better at certain times ① | | In between ③ | | I have difficulty tolerating stress all year round ⑤ |

**Meaning.** There is no such thing as an "ideal" score. Scores greater than 20 suggest high levels of unhealthy tolerance. You could benefit from professional support. Scores less than 10 suggest either (1) you are a highly tolerant person, unaware of stressors that can hurt you, or (2) you have reached a state of serenity. Scores between 11 and 19 suggest that you are engaged in a relatively healthy way and monitor your tolerance fairly well. You may need to seek out support from others (potentially professional support) if your total score is 20 or greater. See Tool #12 on Preventive Help-Seeking.

TOOL #10
Developing a Flexible Window for Tolerance

> Note: Use a personal journal so you have more room to comment. To get the most out of this tool, choose a situation in your life that really bothers you a lot and is testing your limits.

*Purpose:* To investigate your general posture of tolerance as a way to foster openness to new opportunities for resilience. (See Tool #6 on values and Tool #9 on tolerance.)

*Background:* Your tolerance level may be too low (you tolerate too much, feel overwhelmed, like a victim) or too high (you are critical and judgmental, always having to manage things). These extreme positions may bring temporary benefit, but as a basic posture, they can ultimately prevent you from facing challenges to help you grow.

In this tool, steps ❶, ❷, and ❸ help you see your tolerance posture and ❹ introduces the idea of a range of tolerance. You then ❺ review your values, ❻ assess how they inform your tolerance posture, and ❼ challenge yourself to ❽ respond in a skillful way.

❶ In this table list at least three things (persons, situations, ideas) you tolerate and three things you do not tolerate.

| Things I tolerate<br>I put up with and don't respond | Things I don't tolerate<br>I have to respond, do something |
|---|---|
| . | . |
| . | . |
| . | . |

❷ Reflect on a situation where you believe things could be better because some person, group, or system is set in their ways, adhering to behaviors that you believe are harmful or unhealthy. Write at least two items in the four cells in response to these questions: (a) What are the costs for tolerating the situation? (b) What are the potential costs for responding? (c) What are the benefits of responding? (d) What are the benefits of tolerating? (Note: I suggest that you save (d) for your last response because it may be difficult to see or admit to the "pay off" for doing nothing. Completing (a), (b), and (c) beforehand may make this easier.)

|  | Tolerate | Respond |
|---|---|---|
| Costs | a (such as "the problem does not go away")<br><br>•<br>•<br>•<br>• | b (such as "I may hurt someone's feelings")<br><br>•<br>•<br>•<br>•<br>• |
| Benefits | d (such as "I don't have to take any risks")<br><br>•<br>•<br>•<br>• | c (such as "the problem gets solved")<br><br>•<br>•<br>•<br>•<br>• |

❸ Now ask yourself:
   (1) Is it better to tolerate or to respond?
   (2) Can I be more flexible in how I respond to the situation?

❹ Consider the benefits of having a range of tolerance. Some call this knowing when to "pick your battles" and when to "not sweat the small stuff." At any point in your life, your attitudes will vary along a continuum of tolerant ⬅➡ intolerant. Imagine this as a bi-directional arrow with a vertical line at the left end (your bottom-line of what you CAN tolerate ... *the small stuff*) and right end (your top-line of what you MUST respond to ... *your key battles*).

The diagram that follows depicts three imaginary types of positions a person might take. Position A is more tolerant. Position C is more intolerant. Position B is in between.

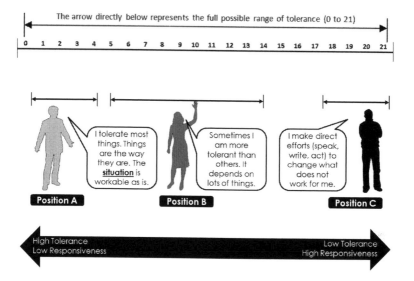

⑤ Reflect on values that inspire you. Examples from Tool #6 include family, security, wealth, achievement, and health. Your values tell you what to take a stand for and those goals that lead you to enjoy and master life. They also tell you what you can accept, what you are willing to let go and those issues that are just not important to you.

⑥ Now, consider your key values, draw an arrow that represents your range of tolerance. Use the following line. "0" = you take a very tolerant and accepting position. "21" = you take a very responsive and action-oriented position. You can draw different arrows for different situations in your life (home, work, politics, for example).

| 0 | 1 | 2 | 3 | 4 | 5 | 6 | 7 | 8 | 9 | 10 | 11 | 12 | 13 | 14 | 15 | 16 | 17 | 18 | 19 | 20 | 21 |

⑦ As you reflect on your arrow, ask yourself:
- Am I being too tolerant such that I avoid taking an action that could lead to new opportunities?
- Am I being too intolerant such that I don't allow myself a new way of seeing things?
- Can I modify my range on this issue in any way?
- Is there some gift that I cannot see right now that will help me grow?

⑧ What is the best, most skillful, most mindful response you can have? (The next tool asks you to further explore a mindful response)

Tool #11

Knowing Your Limits of Strain and Tolerance

*Purpose:* To explore and know your limits for strain.

*Background:* Stress has a four-part definition in *Raw Coping Power* (see Principle #1) which includes the stressor, the strain, and also our responses to these. How we respond to stress shapes its impact on us. This exercise first invites you to examine whether the strain you experience is a function of how you are responding to it. Then it asks you to explore whether you can be more skillful in how you respond.

*Exercise.* Reflect on a situation that is currently causing you strain or an area you are avoiding because you fear it will cause you strain. Now, ask yourself the following series of questions:

1) How much are you tolerating that situation?

2) Are you tolerating it for these reasons:

- Too much trouble to deal with
- Better to not "rock the boat"
- Better to "let sleeping dogs lie"
- I don't know what to do
- I don't have the support I need
- I have a resentment that I have not resolved
- If I addressed the situation, people might get hurt
- Other? _____

3) Can you "let go" of any of these reasons?

4) At what point can you relax and let go?

5) At what point do you say "enough is enough" because tolerating the situation is causing damage to your health or well-being?

After reviewing these questions, ask yourself if there *is any healthy or skillful way that you can respond to the situation*. Review the tolerate-respond grid in the previous tool (and repeated as follows).

- Think about the benefits of responding.
- Explore how you might skillfully respond to the situation so that you address the limits of your strain rather than continue to suffer.
- Is it time for you to take action?
- If not now, when?

| | Tolerate | Respond |
|---|---|---|
| Costs | | |
| Benefits | | Put your focus here. How can you produce benefits by HOW you respond in a mindful and skillful way? |

Tool #12

Preventive Help-Seeking

*Purpose:* To (1) recognize the resilience and thriving benefits of seeking help and support from others, (2) maintain your commitment to receive such help, or (3) reduce or eliminate any judgment or stigma you have about getting help. This includes professional guidance from a counselor, coach, therapist, or employee assistance professional.

*Background:* Several of the previous exercises point to the possibility that you may need to reach out for help. Specifically,

- When you listed stressors in Tool #3, you may have felt overwhelmed by all the stressors in your life.
- When you reviewed your set-point level in Tool #4, you may have realized that *My Level* was too low for your liking.
- When you reviewed your early warning signs in Tool #7, you may have noticed that you have been neglecting yourself for too long.
- When you reviewed your tolerance levels (Tools #9 to #11), you may have realized that your tolerance has cost you too much and now you need help.
- You may have also recognized that you have been too intolerant in ways that did not create a more workable situation for yourself and others. Your intolerance led to actions or a style of communicating that was ineffective, distancing, or self-sabotaging.

*Exercise.* Many different resources are available to you right now through the Internet, your local community (for example, social service agencies supported by the United Way), and possibly through your employer or your spouse's employer. Many workers can access an employee assistance professional to help with a variety of situations, including legal and financial guidance.

The following Internet web-links point to a variety of agencies that can be helpful to you. If you don't see what you are looking for, then consider your local community and employer as resources. Sometimes the information you review via the web is sufficient. Sometimes you will need to make contact via phone or email. Reach out. It's a great coping skill.

| If stress is associated with | You may consider resources at: |
|---|---|
| alcohol problems | Alcoholics Anonymous *www.aa.org* |
| drug problems or risks | Narcotics Anonymous *www.na.org* |
| overeating/weight control | Overeaters Anonymous *www.oa.org* |
| problems taking care of your heart* | American Heart Association *www.heart.org* |
| problems controlling or living with diabetes | American Diabetes Association *www.diabetes.org* |
| mental health problems | National Alliance on Mental Illness *www.nami.org* |
| depression or bipolar disorder | Depression & Bipolar Support Alliance *www.dbsalliance.org* |
| finding treatment | Treatment Locator *www.findtreatment.samhsa.gov* |
| problems with anger | *www.apa.org/topics/anger/control.aspx* |
| Internet addiction | *www.netaddiction.com* |
| sex addiction | *www.slaafws.org* |
| other medical problems or consumer advisory | Medline : *www.nlm.nih.gov/medlineplus/* Medical Library Association *www.mlanet.org/resources/healthlit/* HealthFinder : *www.healthfinder.gov/* |
| potential suicide | *National Suicide Hotline* *www.suicidepreventionlifeline.org/* *1-800-273-TALK (8255)* |
| cancer | *National Cancer Institute* *www.cancer.gov/* |
| children/ teen health | Kids' Health : *http://kidshealth.org/* |
| aging parent's health | National Institute on Aging http://nihseniorhealth.gov/ |

There are also many resources available from www.211us.org.
*Note that chronic stress can also lead to heart disease and heart attacks; please visit WebMD for more information (see stress and heart attack risks). See www.webmd.com/heart-disease/stress-heart-attack-risk. Some chronic stress may also be a function of trauma or post-traumatic stress disorder. See the National Center for PTSD at www.ptsd.va.gov.

## Tool #13
### Knowing Your Later Warning Signs

*Purpose:* To (1) recognize later warning signs that may indicate your situation is more urgent than you previously thought and, if so, (2) take corrective action with a follow-up plan.

*Background:* Early warning signs (your strain signature) tend to be initial signs of strain and are situational. That is, stressors or stressful events lead to your experience of early warning signs, as described in Tool #7. Later warning signs tend to be more chronic and are associated with an ongoing stressful situation or a problem that has been neglected or tolerated for too long. Your set-point can determine whether you tolerate later warning signs.

*Exercise:* There are three parts to this exercise. Part 1 asks you to check all those signs that you have experienced in the past month. Part 2 asks you to think about how many of these signs a person should have before he or she would reach out for help. Part 3 asks you to consider reaching out for help should you have some number of these signs.

*Part 1: Check-In*

*How many of these signs have you had in the past month?*

- [ ] Changes in sleep habits (too much or too little)
- [ ] Changes in eating habits (losing/gaining weight)
- [ ] Unable to shake off feeling blue or down in the dumps
- [ ] Increased use of alcohol or other drugs
- [ ] Feeling like "it's just not worth it"
- [ ] Feeling like "everything is hopeless"
- [ ] Difficulty concentrating; distracted; "in a fog"

☐ Unable to control anger; irritable over "little things"

☐ Crying a lot or "shutting down" your feelings

☐ Fighting with family, friends, coworkers

☐ Bothered by repeated and disturbing dreams

☐ Avoiding reminders of past stress (people, places, activities)

☐ Unable to feel close to others; feel like a stranger

*Part 2: Reflect*

*How many of these do you personally believe an individual should have before he or she needs to stop and realize it is time to get help?*

☐ At least one

☐ At least two

☐ At least three

☐ Four or more

☐ It depends on which signs are involved

☐ It depends on the person

---

REFLECTION

As you reflect on your answer, consider whether it is shaped by your set-point or tolerance level. Some people live with constant stress due to war, disease, catastrophe, poverty, trauma, or violence. In such circumstances, you may think that they can tolerate many later warning signs. However, even in such circumstances, it is those people who recognize their warning signs and take corrective action who are more likely to be resilient and thrive compared to others who just "stomach" or "put up with" the problem.

---

*Is it possible that having just one warning sign*
*is sufficient reason to get help?*

*Part 3: Seek Help*

If you feel you should get help based on Part 2, please review the information from Tool #12 on Preventive Help-Seeking. It may also help you to know that the signs listed in Part 1 are often associated with depression and/or post-traumatic stress disorder (PTSD).

For more resources on depression, please visit www.mentalhealthamerica.net.

For resources on PTSD also consider www.ptsd.va.gov/ with helpful videos at www.ptsd.va.gov/professional/videos/index.asp.

TOOL #14
Set-Point Review

> Note: This tool may be best used with a personal journal so you have more room to comment and explore your responses.

*Purpose:* To review your set-point on an ongoing basis and to maintain vigilance around a healthy level of resilience and thriving.

*Background:* Principle #6 tells us that we can use energy to go beyond resilience to experience flourishing or thriving. Lens #4 on potentiation tells us that we can flourish and thrive even if we have problems such as an addiction, anxiety, depression, a serious disease, or post-traumatic stress disorder. As we all know, life happens! We can experience set-backs from time to time, and we may feel vulnerable because of a health condition.

These previous exercises helped you examine your ability to bounce back as well as flourish and thrive in the face of challenge:

Tool #4 Tapping into your Willingness and Set-Point
Tool #9 Knowing your Tolerance Levels for Strain
Tool #11 Knowing Your Limits of Strain and Tolerance

This next exercise asks you to review your set-point again to see if you can take it to the next level, one step at a time.

*Exercise:* The survey is one you can take as a daily review, especially if you are on a serious program of tapping into more resilience in your life. You may wish to review the survey at least once a week or once a month.

The survey asks: "During the previous day how much time did you spend in each of the different states, moods, or attitudes described below?" You answer from not at all (None) to most of your time (Most). The value of your answer differs for each of the seven areas.

The main point of this exercise is NOT in tabulating your summary score (which will range between -100 and +100). The main point of this exercise is to ask yourself:

*What can I learn from how I lived my life today, from how I responded to situations, so that I can continue growing and taking action in support of my values and raw coping power?*

**During the previous day**, how much time did you spend in each of the different states, moods, or attitudes described in this table?

| | None | Little | Some | Much | Mostly | |
|---|---|---|---|---|---|---|
| **Thriving.** I experienced vitality, fulfillment, and meaning knowing that I was contributing to life, society, and others. | 0 | +5 | +10 | +20 | +30 | |
| **Resilience.** I kept an attitude of confidence despite any challenges or set-backs. | -5 | +5 | +10 | +15 | +20 | |
| **Healthy Coping.** I ate well, exercised, got sufficient rest and coped well (with problem solving, positive self-talk). | -5 | 0 | +5 | +10 | +15 | |
| **Tolerating.** I felt like I just got by, not doing my best but not doing my worst either. | +5 | 0 | -5 | -10 | -15 | |
| **Unhealthy Coping.** I chose unhealthy coping outlets (such as food, avoidance, moodiness, zoning out, negative self-talk). | +10 | -5 | -10 | -15 | -20 | |
| **Addiction.** I did things that I know are unhealthy or addictive habits (such as smoking, drinking, Internet, food). | +10 | -10 | -15 | -20 | -25 | |
| **Distress.** I felt depressed, anxious, worried, or angry; or I was preoccupied with the stress in my life. | +10 | -15 | -20 | -25 | -30 | |
| TOTAL ALL 7 SCORES HERE ➜ | | | | | | |

SCORING

The total score for this survey can range between -100 to +100. You may wish to label or interpret this score in your own way. You can also use the labels to gauge yourself but we recommend finding the meaning that is most helpful to you. Using the labels, a score near 0 would indicate tolerating, positive scores would lead toward resilience and thriving, and negative scores would lead toward more addiction and distress as follows:

| | |
|---|---|
| Thriving | between +70 and +100 |
| Resilience | between +40 and +70 |
| Healthy Coping | between +15 and +40 |
| Tolerating | between -15 and +15 |
| Unhealthy Coping | between - 40 and - 15 |
| Addiction | between -70 and -40 |
| Distress | between -100 and - 70 |

REFLECTION

You may already know that you are not taking good care of yourself or doing the best you can for your health. This set-point review may further make you keenly or even painfully aware of this fact. For now, tell yourself that it is acceptable to have such awareness. For now, view the feedback as an opportunity for a single self-reflection:

I am getting in touch with what I need to do
to nurture my inner guardian and stay wakeful.
With that knowledge, I move forward with my day.

TOOL #15

Adapting the Stress > Evaluate > Cope Framework

> Note: This tool may be best used with a personal journal so you have more room to comment and explore your responses.

*Purpose:* To create the mindset and expectation that you can nurture your own inner guardian and transform stress into opportunities for thriving. This exercise primes or prepares you for the next set of tools (#16 and #17).

*Background:* Lens #6 introduced the stress > evaluate > cope cycle of positive coping. Tool #3 asked you to list your stressors, tell how you cope, and craft an initial statement for your inner guardian (for example, "I am compassionate and ready to greet challenges in my life."). You nurture this guardian through a healthy lifestyle and effective coping styles and positive beliefs.

*Exercise:* In the Evaluate space write your statement from Tool #3. Next, think about one lifestyle factor that supports your inner guardian and write that in the space above (for example, diet, exercise, daily meditation). Think of an effective coping style or positive belief and write that in the space below (some examples are problem solving, deep breathing, getting help). Imagine these resources feed your inner guardian.

Examples to help prompt you:

- Healthy lifestyle factors include eating vegetables, getting sleep, spending time with others who care about you, etc.
- Effective Coping Styles and Beliefs include problem solving, thinking positive thoughts, taking time away to build positive energy, telling yourself that you can work it out, etc.

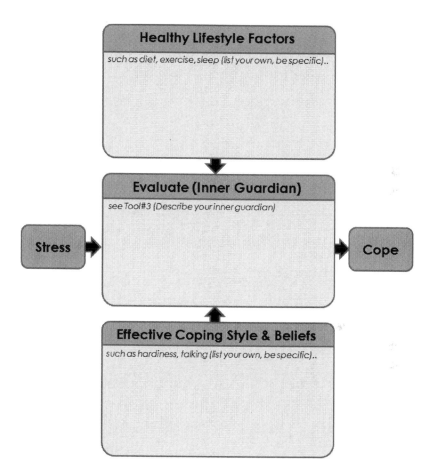

## Tool #16
### Reviewing Your Healthy Lifestyle Factors

*Purpose:* To identify your lifestyle strengths and areas needing further development.

*Background:* Healthy lifestyle factors enhance your ability to choose healthy responses to stress and/or thrive from stress.

*Exercise:* Complete the following survey and then follow the instructions. Keep in mind that higher scores (3 or 4) are always in the positive or healthy direction.

| 1= Very Unlike Me (VUM)    2= Unlike Me (UM)<br>3= Like Me (LM)    4= Very Like Me (VLM) | VUM | UM | LM | VLM |
|---|---|---|---|---|
| 1. I exercise regularly (at least three times a week). | 1 | 2 | 3 | 4 |
| 2. I eat nutritious, balanced meals (high in vegetables, fruits, grains, low in fat and cholesterol) | 1 | 2 | 3 | 4 |
| 3. I maintain a proper weight for my height and age. | 1 | 2 | 3 | 4 |
| 4. I sleep 7 to 8 hours nightly. | 1 | 2 | 3 | 4 |
| 5. I get the proper amount of rest and relaxation. | 1 | 2 | 3 | 4 |
| 6. I do not smoke cigarettes or use tobacco. | 1 | 2 | 3 | 4 |
| 7. I use alcohol in moderation, if at all. | 1 | 2 | 3 | 4 |
| 8. I do not use drugs to get high or feel good about myself. | 1 | 2 | 3 | 4 |
| 9. I give and receive affection with others. | 1 | 2 | 3 | 4 |
| 10. I have friends or family that I can count on. | 1 | 2 | 3 | 4 |
| 11. I practice some form of intentional relaxation (deep breathing, stretching, meditation, prayer) regularly. | 1 | 2 | 3 | 4 |
| 12. Spirituality or religious faith is important in my life | 1 | 2 | 3 | 4 |
| 13. I know how to recognize when I am getting too stressed by a problem or situation. | 1 | 2 | 3 | 4 |

This scale was adapted with permission from Lyle H. Miller and Alma Dell Smith at the Biobehavioral Sciences in Brookline, Massachusetts, and Stress Directions. For more information about their work and a more thorough assessment, visit their website (www.stressdirections.com) or call (617) 738-4814.

## SCORING

Total your scores and write down your Total number.
Note. There are five lifestyle areas or domains shown:
- Diet & Nutrition (Items 1, 2, 3)
- Sleep & Rest (Items 4 and 5)
- Avoiding Substances (Items 6, 7, 8)
- Social Support (Items 9, 10)
- Spirituality and Mindfulness (Items 11, 12, 13)

What do your general scores mean?

| Low = 13 - 21 | Average = 22 - 39 | High = 40 - 52 |
|---|---|---|

This scale assesses personal habits and lifestyle conditions as you move toward, or maintain, health and wellness.

*High* scores indicate that you are using strategies or have life conditions that serve to protect you from developing health problems if and when situations of stress or problems arise. These strategies and conditions also help prevent chronic or ongoing distress.

*Low* scores indicate that there is room for personal development in terms of nurturing a healthy lifestyle. If you scored low, please pay attention to any particular item where you rated a 1 or a 2 and see if you can change something about the situation. If not, call on other strengths you have (ratings of 3 or 4) and effective response strategies (see next exercise).

| What specific steps should you take? |
|---|

Write your response to each of the following four questions.
1. What are your strengths? What specific items do you have 4s in?
2. Where can you improve? What specific items do you have 2s or 1s in?
3. Which of the five domains is your greatest strength? Which is an area needing the most work?
4. What positive step will you take with a specific item and/or with a specific domain you can improve? Write that down:

| STEP I WILL TAKE: |
|---|
|  |

## TOOL #17
## Reviewing Your Coping Style Factors

*Purpose:* To identify your coping style strengths and areas needing further development.

*Background:* Healthy coping style factors enhance your ability to choose healthy responses to stress and/or thrive from stress.

*Exercise:* Think about the more stressful events that have occurred within the recent past. How have you coped with these events? How do you respond to ongoing problems that you encounter? Check all those items that fit with your way of responding to stress.

### Coping Style Factors

| | | | |
|---|---|---|---|
| 1. I seek reassurance from others | ☐ | 16. I withdraw from the situation | ☐ |
| 2. I talk to people to help feel better | ☐ | 17. I avoid being with people in general | ☐ |
| 3. I plan a course of action rather than act on impulse | ☐ | 18. I "take my frustration" out on others (yelling or being snappy) | ☐ |
| 4. I brainstorm possible solutions before deciding what to do | ☐ | 19. I otherwise act aggressively (drive car fast, express anger) | ☐ |
| 5. I typically find the confidence to approach the situation | ☐ | 20. I "zone out," become numb, let my mind just drift (watch TV) | ☐ |
| 6. I affirm myself for positive accomplishments | ☐ | 21. I daydream about better times | ☐ |
| 7. I take things in stride, I know I bounce back from problems | ☐ | 22. I become compulsive (for example, compulsive shopping, eating, exercising, drinking) | ☐ |
| 8. I tend to look on the bright side | ☐ | 23. I eat too much or too little | ☐ |
| 9. I look for ways to take control rather than feel overwhelmed | ☐ | 24. I crave sweets (chocolate, cookies, candy, soda) junk food | ☐ |
| 10. I see situations as challenges to overcome | ☐ | 25. I drink alcohol (beer, wine, liquor) | ☐ |
| 11. I do things to ground or center my body (like deep breathing, yoga, qigong, tai chi) | ☐ | 26. I smoke or chew tobacco | ☐ |
| 12. I exercise or do physical work | ☐ | 27. I drink coffee | ☐ |
| 13. I do activities or hobbies to refresh myself (garden, sport, read, play, take a bath) | ☐ | 28. I use a drug to take the edge off | ☐ |
| 14. I pray, meditate, or do spiritual reading | ☐ | 29. I cry or become very moody | ☐ |
| 15. I try to get extra sleep or rest | ☐ | 30. I get easily exhausted and fatigued | ☐ |

## SCORING

Tally up the number of boxes you checked in column 1 (Items 1–15); Tally up the boxes you checked in column 2 (Items 16–30). Which column has the higher number? Column 1 responses tend to be more effective (positive coping cycle). Column 2 responses are often less effective, especially as habits (negative coping cycle).

This is an index or naming key for the Coping Style Factors

| | | | |
|---|---|---|---|
| 1-2 | social support | 16-17 | withdrawal/avoidance |
| 3-4 | problem solving | 18-19 | aggression |
| 5 | hope | 20-21 | tuning out |
| 6 | self-efficacy | 22 | compulsive behavior |
| 7 | resilience | 23-24 | use food |
| 8 | optimism | 25 | alcohol |
| 9 | sense of control (hardiness) | 26 | tobacco |
| 10 | sense of challenge (hardiness) | 27 | caffeine |
| 11 | body grounding/centering | 28 | drugs |
| 12 | exercise | 29 | emotions |
| 13 | relaxation/healthy hobby | 30 | energy depletion |
| 14 | spirituality | | |
| 15 | energy management | | |

## ADDITIONAL STEPS

*STEP 1.* Please review the list and place a check ☑ next to *all* those activities that you do on a regular basis.

*STEP 2.* Review the list again and circle O those items that you wish to add or improve.

*STEP 3.* Review the list again and ~~cross out those items~~ that you need to reduce or eliminate.

Tool #18

Celebrating Strengths and Choosing a New Goal

*Purpose:* To celebrate the strengths you identified from your review of lifestyle and coping factors and to create a new positive goal in additional areas.

*Background:* Setting new goals is important to continuing your development as a resilient and thriving individual. These goals do not just emerge in a vacuum. Rather, they are based in our strengths and are established from a desire for fulfillment rather than from weakness and a sense of lacking something.

*Exercise:* Please do Part 1 and Part 2.

## Part 1: Celebrate Strengths

Review your strengths from Tools #16 (Lifestyle Review) and #17 (Coping Style Review). Write down your strengths as follows:

- List one specific lifestyle item that you really enjoy.
- Which of the five lifestyle domains is your favorite?
- Which of the effective coping items (1–15) is your favorite?
- Which of the ineffective items (16–30) are you happy to be gone from your life?

Take a minute to reflect on how you have come by these strengths. See yourself as a resilient and thriving person. Celebrate yourself.

NOTE: Share these strengths with a trusted friend, family member, or support person who can appreciate you for your strengths. Ask them if you can do the same for them.

## PART 2: Formulate a New Goal

Select one area from the previous exercises that you want to improve, either a lifestyle or coping factor to enhance. This can be anything from the lists provided or any area you want to work on.

MY NEW GOAL:

TOOL #19
Goal Setting and Positive Intentions Exercise

> Note: This tool may be best used with a personal journal so you have more room to comment and explore your responses. Consider copying the four-step chart located in this tool.

*Purpose:* To learn how to set a specific actionable goal and formulate a specific intention to help you realize that goal.

*Background:* This exercise brings together the three previous exercises (#16, #17, and #18). It asks you to focus on a stress area that you would like to address. The goal is to formulate an actionable intention that you have a realistic chance of implementing. It is possible to actively problem solve. Your job is to specify a first step (when, where, and how). This exercise can actually transform the stressor into a positive factor because you look at the stress in a new way.

*Exercise:* Follow these four steps using columns from the illustration that follows:

1. *Identify the stressor.* Describe a current problem that is causing you to feel stress (perhaps your warning signs).

2. *List positive ways to cope with it.* List one or two effective ways or coping tools to cope with the situation.

3. *Set specific goals to achieve in addressing the stressor.* If you used this coping tool, what goal would you achieve that addresses the stressor (listed in column 1)? This goal is stated in the present and affirmative tense. Form statements that tell your brain that you are already and actively having, being, or doing the goal. Instead of saying, "I will exercise to the point of sweating three times a week," say "I exercise to the point of sweating."

4. *Make specific steps (an intention).* Remember that intention and visualize success. What specific action can you take to achieve that goal; When? Where? How?

Tips to follow when completing this exercise:

- Note that step 4 is really your first step, formulating an intention to actually implement your plan.
- Set out in advance when, where, and how you will achieve this goal. The most effective form for an intention is the if/then format. For example, IF I talk directly to my coworker on Monday and ask for his feedback, THEN I will know that I took that step instead of worrying about it all week.[5]
- Ultimately, you will create a positive statement said in the present tense. Examples are provided before the four-step chart.

| STRESSOR | POSITIVE WAY TO COPE | SPECIFIC GOAL | FIRST STEP* (IF - THEN) |
|---|---|---|---|
| Describe a current problem that is causing you to feel stress (such as early warning signs). | List one or two effective ways that you might cope with the situation. | If you used this coping tool, what goal would you achieve that addresses the stressor (listed in column 1)? | What specific action can you take to achieve that goal; WHEN? WHERE? HOW? |

## EXAMPLES OF GOAL SETTING WITH POSITIVE INTENTION

| STRESSOR | POSITIVE WAY TO COPE | SPECIFIC GOAL | FIRST STEP (IF - THEN) |
|---|---|---|---|

### Example 1: Losing insurance and weight gain

| STRESSOR | POSITIVE WAY TO COPE | SPECIFIC GOAL | FIRST STEP (IF - THEN) |
|---|---|---|---|
| Insurance money for my condition is being withdrawn. I have weight problems and the wellness program is ineffective. | I more assertively communicate my needs with my doctor to help with my weight. I listen and collaborate with my doctor. | *I develop a new strategy for weight control. I am persistent with my doctor and insurance company. My condition is improving.* | **IF** I watch a film about a vegetable juicing program this week **THEN** I will create a plan to get the right ingredients. If I lose weight THEN doctor will write a recommendation. |

### Example 2: Unable to write

| STRESSOR | POSITIVE WAY TO COPE | SPECIFIC GOAL | FIRST STEP (IF - THEN) |
|---|---|---|---|
| I'm anxious about writing; I have to be perfect. I put too much pressure on myself to get it right and I have no one to review my work. | Get started. I see my situation and "JUST START WRITING" without worrying. I tell myself, *This does not have to be all/end all. I can do a decent job on my own.* | *I'm an efficient writer. I am confident. I have a tool that propels my career. I am a valuable provider of written material that helps people.* | **IF** I craft slides for my seminar over the weekend and I feel pressure **THEN** I remind myself to put something on paper and rework it later. I see I am a valuable provider who helps people. |

### Example 3: Boss piles on work at end of week

| STRESSOR | POSITIVE WAY TO COPE | SPECIFIC GOAL | FIRST STEP (IF - THEN) |
|---|---|---|---|
| My boss asks me to do a volume of work that exceeds the number of hours. I sacrifice sleep in order to get it done. This hurts my well-being. | I calculate the number of hours the task will take. I then let my boss know how long this task takes. I set a stop time no matter what. When there are multiple requests (pending), I ask for priorities. | *My needs are as great as my employer's. I am comfortable doing work and other things important to me and my family. Work requests are increasingly realistic. I feel better and I look better.* | **IF** on (Friday afternoon) I get a request for work due on Monday **THEN** I will say: It will take me this many hours, I will start on it this afternoon and I will be able to get it to and provide the product to you by (Wednesday). |

| STRESSOR | POSITIVE WAY TO COPE | SPECIFIC GOAL | FIRST STEP* (IF - THEN) |
|---|---|---|---|
| Describe a current problem that is causing you to feel stress (such as early warning signs). | List one or two effective ways that you might cope with the situation. | If you used this coping tool, what goal would you achieve that addresses the stressor (listed in column 1)? | What specific action can you take to achieve that goal? WHEN? WHERE? HOW? |
|  |  |  |  |

TOOL #20
Mind-Body Infusing of Your Intention

*Purpose:* To incorporate or embody your positive intention into your mind-body framework through visualization and breathing.

*Background:* For many individuals, stating a specific intention with a clear behavioral goal is all that is necessary to start putting that goal into actual practice. To improve these chances, it also helps to create a relaxed mental state and imaginatively embrace the intention as though it were really happening. Create the reality by visualizing it.

*Exercise:* This two-part exercise requires formulating an intention (Tool #18) or first step (Tool #19) and then following this script.

*Part 1: Relaxing with your intentions*
- Bring to mind your statements from your Specific Goal and your First Step. Find a single phrase that you like and make sure to repeat in the positive present tense (I am ..., My needs are ..., I have ...).
- Repeat this statement to yourself quietly and calmly for one minute.
- Sit up straight, feet flat on the floor, imagine a string pulling from the base of your spine through the top of your head.
- Inhale for 6 counts > Exhale for 6 counts.
- Repeat this calm and paced breathing until you are relaxed (about one to three minutes as needed).
- Again, repeat your statement in a calm voice for one minute.

*Part 2: Infusing your intention (see script from Tool #2)*
- Continue to repeat your statement in a calm voice. Imagine the situation unfolding in a positive way. Visualize the who, what, when, where, how and the positive outcome from your statement (for example, "The plan with my doctor is easy to use" or "I calmly put aside my work" or "I feel better and look better.").
- Once that image is in your mind, repeat the script from Tool #2: My arms and legs are heavy and warm • My heartbeat is calm and regular • My breathing is free and easy • My abdomen is warm • My forehead is cool • My mind is quiet and still.
- Open your eyes and take a moment to get oriented. Do something that moves you immediately in the direction of your goal.

TOOL #21
Follow-up: Sharing, Reminders, Relapse Management

*Purpose:* To review the Stress > Evaluate > Cope (SEC) model, share any learning or insights you had with others, create reminders for yourself, and manage stress when you relapse into old patterns.

*Background:* The exercises on the SEC model (Tools #15 through #19) made you personally familiar with three ideas: (1) you can choose how to respond to stress, (2) you can nurture your inner guardian to make the best choices, and (3) you can craft specific intentions to strengthen this habit. Now review this diagram of the SEC model, paying attention to the arrows in the model.

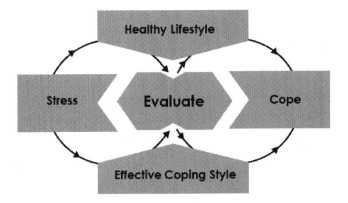

The arrows indicate that evaluation is an ongoing process: how you process stress (experience it in your mind and body) depends upon your lifestyle and coping style, and these two factors also shape how you cope with the stress. Moreover, with a healthy lifestyle and effective coping styles you better evaluate your situation and set goals and intentions that help you cope, thrive, and flourish.

Of course, knowing all this is not enough. That is, don't expect to improve just by doing the exercises. Follow-up is necessary. There are many wonderful self-help courses and retreats that you can attend for a day, a week, or more. You can have great insights from these, but if you don't apply them back in the real world, you will not realize the true benefits of your efforts. Similarly, the insights you may have gleaned from the preceding exercises may be very helpful, but, to make the most of it, three additional follow-up activities will help.

*Exercise:* You can do any one or all three of the following. The more you do, the better.

## Part 1: Sharing

Consider any or all of the following ways to share the exercises and your responses to them with others.

- Ask a friend to listen as you reveal insights, benefits, or struggles you have around issues of stress and resilience.
- Make copies of surveys from Tools #16 (Lifestyle) and #17 (Coping Style) and share with others, asking them to complete as well. Begin by telling them what you discovered as your top strengths and let them know the areas you are working on.
- After doing work on your goals and intentions, share any positive steps you took and your current progress.

## Part 2: Reminders

The preceding exercises ask you to write down key statements or ideas. Also, the 7 Principles and 10 Lenses include many brief ideas that are hopeful reminders on the path of resilience. Start creating *Raw Coping Power* messages to yourself: through emails, Post-it notes, self-sent calendar invites, or self-designed collages with pictures. Be creative! You can have fun crafting your own reminder through artwork, use of symbols or inspiring reminders, and affirming messages that you print on a small rock or a coffee or tea mug, or bury somewhere in your closet or drawers at home.

## Part 3: Relapse Management

A relapse is a set-back or return (usually temporary) to a previous unhealthy behavior. It is important to understand that the process of resilience is actually defined by relapse. There would be no "bounce back" without a relapse.

The key is in recognizing that these lapses are part of the process. When they occur, just use your *Raw Coping Power* tools. Three other things to keep in mind:

1. You may feel that you have gotten over a situation or handled a stress. Then, one day, something triggers an old reaction. Remember: No one is perfect. Use the SEC model.
2. Review your strengths from Tools #16 and #17. Make sure that you practice at least one strength immediately and daily thereafter as soon after you recognize the relapse.
3. Take a closer look at the tolerance tools (#9 through #11). Relapses can occur because we have not responded to a situation and the tolerance levels get too high.

TOOL #22
Focus on the Positive: Generating Uplifts[6]

*Purpose:* To remind yourself to focus on, appreciate, and have gratitude for the daily positive events (uplifts) that occur and to actually generate them through attention and attitude.

*Background:* Broadly speaking, two types of stress-related events can occur: major life events and minor daily hassles. Within each type, there are events that can cause a stress reaction, and there are events that can lead to positive well-being. The typical names for these are *major life stressor* versus a *conversion* or *peak experience* and a minor *hassle* versus an *uplift*. Hassles are irritating, frustrating, and distressing. Uplifts enhance our mood and can be feeling joy from receiving affection, relief at hearing good news, or the pleasure of a good night's rest. You know something is an uplift when it leads you to feel well, hopeful, optimistic, effective, or resilient.

*Exercise:* Review the list of uplifts. Which of these can you do now? Which can you bring about in the next hour or next day? Your assignment: generate at least one uplift in the next twenty-four hours.

| | |
|---|---|
| • Chatting and sharing a joke | • Daydreaming |
| • Being in nature | • Sex |
| • Finding something you lost | • Going for a walk |
| • Practicing a hobby | • Solving a problem |
| • Getting enough sleep | • Visit with friendly neighbors |
| • Eating out | • Taking your time |
| • Reading | • Giving/receiving a compliment |
| • Playing a game | • Cutting down on a bad habit |
| • Shopping | • Cooking |
| • Enjoying the weather | • Volunteering |
| • Relaxing | • Calling an old friend |
| • Receiving a note or message | • Noting you have enough money |
| • Being with children | • Traveling or commuting |
| • Finding meaning in life | • Having someone listen to you |
| • Prayer | • Sharing in a chore |
| • Meditation | • Bring or listen for good news |
| • Eating | • Winning something |

## TOOL #23
## Paired Uplift Exercise

*Purpose:* To generate uplifts with another person and reinforce or create a positive social environment.

*Background:* Three lenses look at the world as a fellowship, community, or opportunity to build resilience for others. These lenses are Team Awareness, Team Resilience, and the *We* in Wellness.

We can deepen our experience of community through sharing the benefits of our own personal work and through sharing other tools. This includes sharing your resilience story (Tool #1) doing a mind-body practice (such as yoga or Tai Chi) with others (Tool #2) seeking help (Tool #12), and sharing insights from your work in *Raw Coping Power* (Tool #20). This next exercise specifically involves you working with another to build resilience.

*Exercise:* We recommend a pen and paper or some way to record the list that you generate from this experience. First, copy or show the list of uplifts from the previous exercise. Then follow the instructions. Read together with your partner:

1. "Uplifts are positive experiences that lead us to feel hopeful, optimistic, effective, or resilient ... or to just feel good. We are going to work together to generate a list of uplifts from our lives. Events that have recently occurred or are about to happen. It helps to be brief but also specific (sharing what, when, where)."
2. "We are a team with five minutes to share uplifts with each other. We will take turns, one after the other. Only sharing one uplift at a time. One of us will write down each uplift as it is shared." [Five minutes is recommended so we can keep it simple and start experiencing more uplifts in our lives!]
3. "Each uplift has to be unique and not the same as what the previous partner just said. So, if one of us says "listening to music," the other will come up with something else, such as "eating out."
4. "At the end, we are going to count the number of uplifts that we have, and then we will share."

After you have your list, post it online (Facebook, Twitter) or share in an email or group of friends and invite them to do the same.

TOOL #24
## Visualization: Future Self for Efficacy, Hope, Optimism [7]

*Purpose:* To visualize yourself as a strong resilient person and to embody that vision as part of who you are—your basic being.

*Background:* This exercise is probably the most involved of all because it brings together different tools into one experience. It takes a few minutes (up to thirty) the first time through. After that, it takes just a few minutes. You can practice it regularly to prepare you for challenges, or you can also do it as a daily warm up. The graphic explains the steps in the exercise to help prepare you.

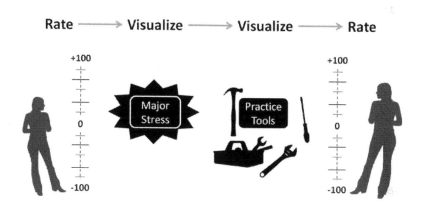

*Exercise:* The exercise has four parts as follows:

*PART 1: SET-POINT PREVIEW*

1.  First, you will need to review Tool #14 (Set-Point Review) and take the survey there. You have to be really honest with yourself when you are under stress: in your mind, in your body, emotionally, and socially. Then rate yourself being as honest as you can. Use the scale -100 to +100. Write down your number. This is not a rating of fail-succeed or win-lose. You can fail or lose and still thrive. In fact, most thrivers are those who have lost or failed.

2.  Ask yourself how many days can you live your life at a level of -60 (that's a negative 60) or below before either getting sick or something worse happens.
3.  Okay, what about 10 or below? How many days can you get by?
4.  In the exercise that we are about to do, you are going to visualize yourself under significant stress and rate yourself again.

## PART 2: VISUALIZE STRESS AND TOOL PRACTICE

1.  First, picture yourself in the future working with some job or life challenge, something that you barely tolerate, a real problem.
2.  Imagine, sense, and see where you are with it, your actions, and how your body is reacting. Take a minute to do that.
3.  Now select one or more of the following tools and imagine yourself in that same future situation. This time you see yourself practicing that tool in the situation. Instead of tolerating it, you are practicing.

    - Tool #8: Breathe into and through your strain. Try it for a moment. Be aware of the strain, the warning signs, wherever the tension is. Be mindful of all that and breathe.
    - Tool #11: Develop a range for tolerance. Now find the most beneficial response. Focus on the benefits of responding and see yourself choosing a positive action.
    - Tool #17: Review your coping style. Now choose an effective positive coping activity whatever it might be.
    - Tool #21: Generate an uplift. Think about other positive uplifts that you can have before, during, or after the event.

## PART 3: VISUALIZE TRANSFORMING STRESS

1.  Before proceeding, imagine yourself having effectively applied the tool within the stressful situation.

    - First, notice who you are with, what is happening, what is stressful about the situation, how your body is reacting.
    - Second, notice how you now respond by effectively using the tool(s) from the second part of this exercise. Notice how you are more relaxed, how your response effectively deals with the

stress, how the situation improves or resolves, and other benefits that occur because you are resilient. Notice even that you thrive and flourish in the situation such that what was previously a stressor is now a challenge that you overcame for the benefit of yourself and others.

2.   Now, rate yourself on these three items.

| | | A good deal | Mostly | Greatly | Quite definitely |
|---|---|---|---|---|---|
| 1.  I can find my way out of a problem. | Some ○ | ○ | ○ | ○ | ○ |
| 2.  I am optimistic about my ability to handle is-sues. | Some ○ | A good deal ○ | Mostly ○ | Greatly ○ | Quite definitely ○ |
| 3.  I have the ability to get through challenges. | Some ○ | A good deal ○ | Mostly ○ | Greatly ○ | Quite definitely ○ |

These three items represent increases in (1) confidence, (2) optimism, and (3) self-efficacy.

## PART 4: SET-POINT REVIEW

Now, go back to your set-point rating (from - 100 to +100) and make another rating. The only requirement is that your new rating has to be higher than the rating you provided in Part 1, unless you started with a score of 100!

---

### Notes

As you do these four parts, you will articulate a sense of yourself in the future. This could be an image, a sensation, or a clear or vague sense of yourself with some future stress. You are picturing yourself as someone who has decisively raised your set-point. It can be helpful to write down any thoughts or feelings you have about yourself in this imagined future scenario.

This is a great exercise to do just before going to sleep and when you just wake up. It helps you create a new mental model of yourself, and doing the exercise in a relaxed mental state can make it more effective.

TOOL #25
Job Crafting[8]

*Purpose:* To craft your job at work so it is less stressful, more fulfilling, and supports your resilience journey.

*Background:* The workplace can be a significant source of stress in your life. Even if you effectively use all the tools in this book, you may still face certain unchangeable stressors of your job—things you tolerate. These include heavy work load, monotony, lack of job control or clarity, downsizing, poor or unsupportive supervision, lack of teamwork, among others.

Research suggests that effective workplace-based strategies for stress management include tools that individuals can use as well as organizational or environmental strategies that seek to improve workplace communication and environments. You may not have control over many of these workplace factors. However, you might be able to influence your particular job in such a way that it is less stressful. You can find ways to influence your job with job crafting.

*Exercise:* This exercise has two parts. Part 1 prepares you for Part 2.

## PART 1: LEARN ABOUT JOB CRAFTING

### About Job Crafting

- Many jobs are quite flexible, and their focus can be adjusted to fit the skills and preferences of each employee.
- Job crafting helps you play up your strengths and thus improve performance and satisfaction.
- The emphasis shifts to a focus on the things that you do well (your strengths) rather than areas of weaker performance.
- The good news is that almost any job can be crafted!

## Job Crafting Benefits—Why Do It?

1. Boost results (makes you more efficient at work)
2. Increase enjoyment (find new ways to do what you love)
3. Build skills (helps to be more creative)
4. Increase general ability to cope with work

## 4 Basic Steps for Crafting Your Job

1. Decide what you want to change.
2. Evaluate how the change will impact you and your work environment.
3. Act to put positive change in place.
4. Check on progress, adjust and continue.

## Three Different Forms of Job Crafting

1. *Alter the boundaries...*
   of the job by taking on more or fewer tasks, expanding or diminishing the tasks, or changing how tasks are performed.
   Hint: Many workers find ways to pace tasks, schedule tiny mini-breaks, take brief walks. There is always a way and these add to productivity.
2. *Change relationships...*
   at work by altering the nature or extent of interactions with other people. Hint: It is not always helpful to just simply avoid people as a way to change relationships. You can find ways to reduce your interactions or keep them focused only on simple tasks or things you can manage.
3. *Cognitively change...*
   the job by altering how tasks are perceived.

## PART 2: USE A JOB CRAFTING TOOL

One way to job craft is with these five steps: List, Pick, Rate, Act, and Check. There are other approaches you can use and this is not a "one time only" activity. You may have different aspects of your job, doing different tasks at different times, or working with different people. You can use the five steps with each of these job aspects.

## Step 1. LIST

LIST three aspects (tasks or features) of your job that you enjoy or that make you feel effective.

- _____
- _____
- _____

## Step 2. PICK

PICK one of these aspects that, if you improve/focus on, will have an enhanced or positive effect on you and the workplace. Circle 1, 2, or 3 from Step 1 or write a new aspect in the following space.

## Step 3. RATE

To craft your job to be even better, *RATE* the degree of how much you will change it in each of these areas. Your total score for the three items should be at least 2. If it is less than a 2, see if you can find another job aspect that you may work on (repeat Steps 1 and 2). Use this 4-point scale to make your ratings (N, c, C, C+).

N =       No Plan to Change (0)
c =       I will Change a minor feature in this area (1)
C =       I will Change one important feature in this area (2)
C+ =      I will make a major change in this area (3)

| | N | c | C | C+ |
|---|---|---|---|---|
| I plan to *alter the boundaries* of my job by taking on more or fewer tasks, expanding or diminishing the tasks, or changing how tasks are performed. | 0 | 1 | 2 | 3 |
| I plan to *change relationships* at work by altering the nature or extent of interactions with others. | 0 | 1 | 2 | 3 |
| I plan to *cognitively change* the job by altering how I perceive my tasks (or my attitude toward them). | 0 | 1 | 2 | 3 |

## Step 4. ACT

What exactly will you do? Here is a list of some ideas to get you started but create your own. Pick one that you can commit to.

- ❑ I clean my work area.
- ❑ I focus my time on core tasks and avoid distractions.
- ❑ I pace my work out.
- ❑ I take a healthy lunch break each day.
- ❑ I discuss possible changes in my job or organization with my supervisor.
- ❑ I make a to-do list to feel as if I am accomplishing things.
- ❑ I ask for help from others.
- ❑ I organize my work in such a way to make sure that I do not have to concentrate for too long a period at once.
- ❑ When at home, I notice thoughts about job-related problems and redirect my attention to the present and things I value at home.
- ❑ I develop myself professionally.
- ❑ I delegate when I can to those who may help.
- ❑ I make my work more challenging by examining the underlying relationships between aspects of my job.
- ❑ I think about accomplishments I have made throughout my career.
- ❑ OTHER: _____

## Step 5. CHECK

Check on your commitments in the previous list, evaluate your progress, then make adjustments and continue. Every day or week you can go back to step 1 and cycle through to keep refining and making things better.

TOOL #26

Five Cs of Resilience

*Purpose:* Use the Five Cs of resilience as a map to explore and identify your own unique meaning of resilience.

*Background:* Lens #5 claims that there are five core competencies of resilience: Centering, Confidence, Community, Commitment, and Compassion. These five terms are abstract categories. As single words, they may not help you get in touch with your own inner resilience: What does resilience really mean to you? The following exercise helps you get in touch with your own unique understanding of resilience and empowers you to craft your own meaning.

Resilience is also both a mind and a body process. Words alone may not convey its true meaning. Also, some of us are more body-oriented than mind-oriented. Language can prevent us from accessing messages that our body sends us that we resonate with.

The following exercise helps you identify your personal resilience in two ways. First, I list sentences to review. These are not a survey to rate because the goal here is to help you find your own meaning rather than rate or score resilience. Then I want you to reflect on various words and phrases that are synonymous with or associated with each of the Five Cs. Use both exercises together or in any way you wish.

*Exercise.* First, assess how much you agree, identify, or resonate with each of the twenty phrases. Is there one C that stands out more than others? Which combination of phrases is most important to you? Then meditate on each of the Five C areas and come up with your own word or phrase for each. You can use any word(s) you wish, whether or not it is shown in the boxed diagram. Following both exercises, ask yourself, *What does resilience really mean to me?* Journal whatever answer comes forth. Paste sticky notes of key terms to your mirror.

| Centering |
|---|
| I have healthy coping skills that give me perspective on life. |
| I know how to slow down and take a break when I need to. |
| My coworkers and I work at an even pace, not rushed to deadlines. |
| I am more likely to pause and take a breath rather than react strongly if someone says something that irritates or angers me. |

| Confidence |
|---|
| People I know would consider me competent and self-assured. |
| I can handle most problems that come my way. |
| People at work believe that their work is important. |
| Faith and inner strength have helped me get through difficult times. |

| Community |
|---|
| There is at least one person in my life whom I can tell my troubles to. |
| I have others who care for and support me. |
| People at work communicate well with each other. |
| During stressful times, I spend at least some time getting support from others rather than withdrawing and trying to "go it alone." |

| Commitment |
|---|
| When difficulties arise, I persist in solving things rather than giving up easily. |
| My life has been a story where I have pursued the dreams and values that are important to me. |
| My coworkers and I can accomplish what we set our minds to. |
| I am a loyal and dedicated person in at least one area in my life (in such roles as a spouse, parent, religious participant, or employee). |

| Compassion |
|---|
| I recall a time recently where I helped someone who was going through a hardship or life problem. |
| It is easy for me to feel pain or upset when someone I care about has similar feelings. |
| People at work show concern when problems happen in our families or wider community. |
| People I know consider me a kind, generous, or sympathetic person. |

## *What does resilience really mean to me?*

relaxed  focused  takin' a break
present  inward  coping  reflecting
**"breathe easy"** meditate  calm
concentrate self-care acceptance
# Centering
vacation **solitude** MANAGING tranquil
unwind  slow down  *settle back*
decompress ease **prayer** revitalized
**'take it easy'** hang loose recline
calm down **refreshed** "chillin"

caring  help  generous  **grace**
supportive reaching out kindness
BENEVOLENT  lending a hand
sympathy friendly humanitarian
# Compassion
hug **generous** NUDGE ALONG forgive
hospitality assist *SELFLESS* befriend
**kind-hearted** comforting **charity**
**goodness** empathy accommodate
loving **encourage** tender-hearted

support  meeting discussion
neighborhood area village commune
**kinship** unity identity spirit
cooperation team convergence
# Community
solidarity **gathering** "US" age-group
ethnic-group network *Social Media*
commonwealth club **family**
**coming together** "work it out"
fellowship **union** commons

COMPETENT effective **hopeful**
optimistic  hardiness  positive focus
FAITH courageous knowledgeable BOLD
assured *willing* assertive reliable
# Confidence
determined **confronting** TOUGH
certainty firmness *FEARLESS* fierce
re-assuring nerve **backbone**
**brave** audacious "look in the face"
adventurous **gutsy** lion-hearted

goal-oriented PLANFUL **achieving**
problem-solving forward-thinking deliberate
PERSEVERE dedicated follow the dream
promise-keeper diligent decisive
# Commitment
sense of purpose handshake invested
responsible loyal *DEVOTED* mission
CALLING **follow-through**
**deliver** sworn **carry out** "take oath"
persist **Vow** clear direction EMPOWERED

*What does resilience really mean to me?*

TOOL #27
Thrive Mapping⁹

Note: This tool may be best used with a personal journal so you have more room to comment and explore your responses. Consider copying the graphic of the thrive map located in this tool.

*Purpose:* To develop your ability to thrive in future situations, to transform your identity as someone who can leverage the very best positive outcomes from even the most difficult of situations. (Those situations may include your own negative coping cycle, an addiction, or poor health habits).

*Background:* To thrive means we feed on the present moment as an opportunity for future growth. How audacious is that? Any experience of adversity improves the future. Adversity, when approached in a skillful way, creates an opportunity for growth—to be better off (stronger, happier, smarter) after the experience than if we had never had the adversity to begin with.

Further, as a result of such growth we are now better equipped to deal with problems. This is a positive adaptation! We now enter into new situations that we previously shied away from. We even attract challenges as opportunities that force us to exercise newfound strengths.

> How would your life be different (in small ways and entirely) were you to thrive at your highest possible level?

As traditionally understood, thriving occurs when we grow not just from the past but are currently, continually, and optimistically moving into the future. The thriving self is always transforming the present moment into something positive in the future.

This exercise is similar to Tool #23 in that it asked you to imagine or re-visualize your approach to stressors and see them as opportunities. Tool #23 asked you to reframe a tolerable situation and thrive as a result. In contrast, the current tool asks you to reflect on how your life would be entirely different if you were to thrive. How can you move past coping and bouncing back (resilience) and actually leverage your life—and all its challenges—as something you wholeheartedly embrace with audacity?

*Exercise.* This exercise asks you to create a visual map by writing your responses to a series of questions into spaces on that visual map. You can use this exercise in any situation. Here we ask you to recall your own negative coping cycle, where you failed to activate your guardian (your inner evaluator) and used ineffective coping techniques. If you have difficulty recalling that situation, review Tool #17, items 16 through 30.

This exercise has three parts. For Part 1, recall that stressful situation and your negative coping and write your former reactive and ineffective actions in the visual map. For Part 2, take another look at that situation and revise it by changing how you responded to it. In other words, go back, re-visualize your past, and now choose a response while centered with your inner guardian, a response that reflects your vision and your values. Again, enter your answers in the map. For Part 3, you will affirm to yourself that you have the ability to see yourself as a thriver.

*Part I: Name the Previous Negative Cycle Situation*

Select the previous negative situation. Recall how your body felt. Answer these questions in the map.

1. What caused you stress?
2. How did you react?
3. How well did you evaluate? What did you DO and NOT do?

## Part II: Revise the Situation from the Perspective of Thriving

Put yourself back in that situation and relax as much as you can in an attempt to revise it. Answer these questions briefly.

4.  If you were to change one thing (within your sphere of control) what would you have done differently?

    a) What specific actions could you take to re-center yourself in your inner guardian or otherwise focus on your raw coping power?
    b) After getting re-centered, what would you do to evaluate the situation differently? How can you reframe it?

5.  From this new vantage point, answer these questions:

    a) How can you actually thrive (flourish, grow, become better) because of this stressful event?
    b) Though the stressful situation is difficult, what is the new growth opportunity it is leading to?

6.  If you thrive, what would the new outcome be? How would your life be positively different rather than one where you react and succumb to stress?

## Part III: Affirm your Thriving, Audacious self

Now it's time to identify qualities or traits that you have that make you thrive and how your life situation has current features and qualities that help you to thrive. Review your response to questions 5 and 6. Now, in your mind, act as if those things you wrote are actually and actively occurring now in your life. Answer these questions briefly in the map.

7.  I am able to thrive when I get in touch with these personal qualities and resources (list them).
8.  When I operate from these personal qualities and resources, my situation (environment, others around me) improves in the following ways (list them).

## Part I. Name the Previous Negative Cycle Situation

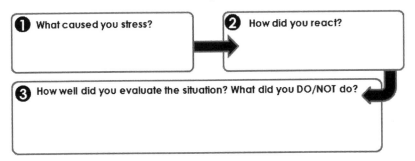

**1** What caused you stress?

**2** How did you react?

**3** How well did you evaluate the situation? What did you DO/NOT do?

## Part II. Revise the Situation from the Perspective of Thriving

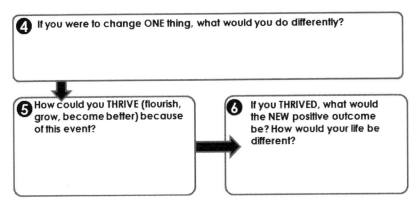

**4** If you were to change ONE thing, what would you do differently?

**5** How could you THRIVE (flourish, grow, become better) because of this event?

**6** If you THRIVED, what would the NEW positive outcome be? How would your life be different?

## Part III. Affirm Your Thriving Self (for all future situations)

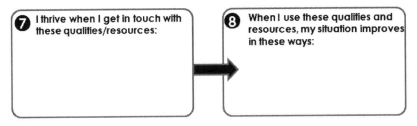

**7** I thrive when I get in touch with these qualities/resources:

**8** When I use these qualities and resources, my situation improves in these ways:

TOOL #28

Work-Life Borders[10]

*Purpose:* To adopt the perspective that you have space or borders between various work-life activities. You can spend time just being in those borders rather than having to strike a balance between activities.

*Background:* Work-life *balance* usually means having personal time for enjoyment of self, friends, and family and ensuring you have time for life as well as work. Work-life *borders* is a more creative way to look at the situation.

Every day we DO different things in different spheres of our lives. The personal sphere includes doing such things as activities at home, performing chores, exercising, hanging out with family or friends.

There is also a work sphere and, for some of us, the school sphere. Some of us also have a community sphere or, because it is a major preoccupation, a financial sphere. In other words, we spend our days traveling across, to and fro, between work, life, community, and so on.

Imagine that our situation is actually quite different. Imagine that most of our life is spent BEING in the BORDER ZONE between all of these spheres. We have only been led to believe that we have to strike a work-life *balance* because our culture emphasizes DOING rather than BEING. In fact, we just have to tap into our purpose in life and BE: relax with the sense that our life—who we really are—is bigger than these spheres or the activities we do inside them.

This next exercise asks you to simply remember, get back in touch with, or imagine your real dream in life. What is your calling? What cause do you have passion about? What legacy do you wish to leave? What is your highest aspiration? Your ideal future? Your vision?

*Exercise.* Review the diagram. Imagine you are bigger than, or have space for, all the various spheres of your life. You have a spacious border that rests between all these spheres. Your life need not be defined by any sphere because you always have time to just rest in that border.

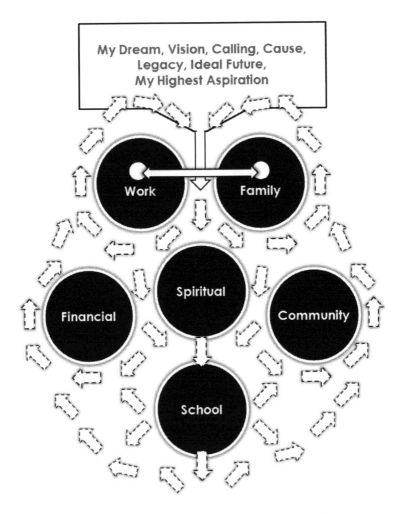

Imagine that every day you remember your real dream in life. This is who you are. As a result, you are less preoccupied with crossing in and out of spheres (such as work-to-life, life-to-work). Instead, everything that happens is coming from a higher or deeper source of BEING that transcends your DOING. Every day you have time to remember that.

### Instructions

First, think about your dreams and aspirations (top of the diagram). Imagine that those shape, influence, or inform the spheres and borders of your life.

Second, adopt the perspective that your life is spent in three ways: (1) doing activities in the borders **between** the work and family spheres, (2) **crossing** between those borders, or (3) doing activities **within** a sphere. As you go about your day, note how you can flow among all the times, places, and situations and tap into the private border that surrounds all spheres of activity.

This includes walking between activities, driving or any type of commuting, preparing a meal, getting ready to leave or arrive somewhere, moving from sitting to standing, looking out the window, getting ready to open a book, and so on. You can access this border and rest there even if only for a moment. This moment refreshes you totally.

Tool #29
Visualization: Building Your Centering Protective Shield

Note: Consider having a journal with you so that you can write down your thoughts and insights after completing this exercise.

*Purpose:* To embrace stress as part of life alongside many different strengths that you bring to any situation. To see stress in perspective and reduce any feelings of overwhelm, anxiety, or worry.

*Background:* Visualization helps us to learn concepts in a new way that can integrate mind, breath, and body together. When we know we are going into a situation that may produce stress and anxiety, it helps us to visualize ourselves handling the situation with poise and serenity. We can actually create our own "protective shield" that helps us minimize stress and keep ourselves from blowing things out of proportion.

You can do this exercise every day or just before entering a difficult situation. Many of the previous concepts and tools come together in this exercise to help you build this protective shield. Lenses 6 and 7 talked about stress > evaluate > cope and the positive and negative coping cycle. This exercise protects you from the negative coping cycle. It also follows from Tool #20, where you reviewed the stress > evaluate > cope model. This time, you put that model into action through visualization.

*Exercise.* Prepare for this next exercise by getting into a comfortable position and establishing deep breathing for a minute or two. Study the following image as an initial map to prepare you for the exercise. However, during the exercise you will focus on the second image of the protective shield without using any of the labels.

Healthy Lifestyle

Stress

Thrive

Positive Beliefs

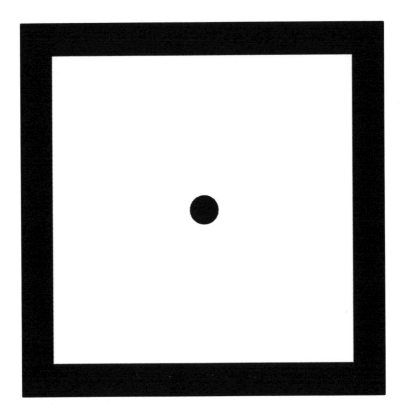

## Step 1

After a minute of quiet and deep breathing, open your eyes and look at the square image in front of you. Imagine that this is also surrounding you and is providing you with protection from life stress. Take a moment to look at each side of the square and then bring your attention to the center dot.

Take one minute for each of the following steps.

## Step 2

Visualize, imagine, sense, and feel any stressor that is in your life right now or create an image or symbol of stressors in your life.

[Place that image, symbol, or feeling to your left.]

*Step 3*

Visualize, imagine, sense, and feel any habits in your life that are strengths for you (diet, exercise, relaxation, taking time for prayer, meditation, social support). Acknowledge to yourself with good feeling your lifestyle strengths. Really recognize that you have these good qualities and capacities within yourself.

[Place that image, symbol, or feeling above you.]

*Step 4*

Recall your positive personal beliefs about yourself: positive self-talk, positive coping styles, problem solving, hardiness, resilience skills. Whatever they are, acknowledge to yourself with good feeling that you have these.

[Place that image, symbol, or feeling below you.]

*Step 5*

Visualize, imagine, sense, and feel any tools you have for positive coping and positive unwinding or create an image or symbol of that positive thriving skill in your life.

[Place that image, symbol, or feeling to your right.]

*Step 6*

Close your eyes and imagine that you are in the center of the square you just imagined. Visualize the stress to your left, positive habits above you, positive personal beliefs below you, and your positive thriving skills to your right. As you sit there, quietly feel gratitude and serenity for being able to be with all of this in your life.

*Closure*

After completing steps 1 through 6, bring back into your mind all the ideas, insights, and feelings that you have learned and integrate that learning. Use a journal to record your thoughts. The learning you receive each time you practice this exercise increases your ability to adapt to situations and enhances your ability to courageously face challenges. Also, you may, with self-compassion, accept the gifts of the exercise and allow them to become part of your wise mind knowing you have a renewed ability to cope, thrive, and/or flourish.

*Just*

*Realize*

*that you are going through a positive cycle:*

*Encounter a problem.*
*Use the tools.*

*Tap into your*
*inner guardian:*

*Learn.*
*Grow.*
*Thrive.*
*Flourish.*

*Have gratitude*
*for opportunities*
*so nourished.*

TOOL #30
Managing Stressful Communication: Really Listening

*Purpose.* With the intention of reducing stress, practice really listening, receiving support, and offering support.

*Background.* A great deal of stress is brought about by poor communication. This means any one of several things: speaking before we think, speaking in anger, failure to consider the other's perspective, rushing to judgment, not paying attention, only focusing on one's own needs, impatience, and holding on to past hurts. Most, if not all, of these factors can be addressed by taking the time to just deeply listen in conversation.

It helps to practice Really Listening when you are not in a stressful situation and to practice it as often as possible with anyone at any time. The more you practice this exercise, the better prepared you are when relationship or communication conflict arises. When you take the time to really relax and listen to another and create an atmosphere of shared support, you can actively tap into your raw coping power.

*Exercise:* Of course, this exercise requires two or three individuals. If doing this with three people, the third person becomes an observer and then the listener and receiver roles shift around so everyone plays each role at least once. The observer provides feedback on how well the listener followed the listening guidelines (Step 2). Becoming familiar with the guidelines in steps 1 and 2 is the key to the success of this exercise.

*Step 1.* Agree on the basic safety guidelines (CHAT)

- *C for Confidentiality:* You all agree that what is shared remains private and confidential and that you will not repeat what you heard again outside of this one-time exercise.

- *H for Honor:* You agree to follow the listening guidelines below that show you honor each other's time. Give your full respect and attention when it is someone else's time to speak.
- *A for Anonymity:* You agree that when sharing you will not use the name or other identifying information of others in your story. This way you protect others. Do not use this time to blame or victimize someone else.
- *T for Trust:* You agree that everyone gets equal time to share without interruption.

*Step 2.* Review these listening guidelines

- Actively listen.
- Listen with concern and respect.
- Don't interrupt the speaker.
- Use brief prompts if you miss something; request clarification ("Can you repeat that?" or "What do you mean by … ?").
- Restate what was said using similar but not exactly the same language to show that you have paid attention and reflect.
- Listen with an open mind whether or not you agree with what the other person has to say.
- If the person becomes emotional, maintain a quiet and steady attitude. Breathe …
- When restating, use a calm, level tone of voice.
- Maintain eye contact.
- Be PRESENT! Avoid showing irritation, angry gestures, or distraction. Breathe….

*Step 3.* Take turns sharing on a selected topic

Agree on a set amount of time to share. Typically, five to ten minutes each. The prime rule is this:

---
**Each person can speak only after restating the ideas and opinions of the previous speaker, accurately and to that speaker's satisfaction.**
---

- Someone should volunteer to begin the discussion by talking briefly about his or her thoughts and opinions about the chosen topic.
- When you want to give your ideas on the topic, you must first show the previous speaker that you got his or her meaning.

You can say things like, "You believe that ..." or "You think that ...", or "Your opinion is that ..." to get started. Then use your own words to restate what you heard the previous speaker say. If the previous speaker is satisfied that you got his or her meaning, then you can give your opinion.

- Say thank you when your turn as a sharer is complete and you feel listened to. Then give positive feedback on how your listener did.

### Topics
Use this list of topics for discussion. You can choose these or create one that you are all comfortable with.

- Is there stress you all face together and how can you cope?
- What do you think should be done to reduce stress?
- What is the most personally stressful event that you have grown from recently?
- What negative coping habit have you had in the past but have now overcome?
- Which of the Five Cs of resilience are most important to you and why (Compassion, Centering, Commitment, Community, or Confidence)?
- Aspects of your job that you plan to address through job crafting. Explain the problem and what you want to change.
- Recall a time when you sought professional or spiritual help. Why did you do so? What was the outcome?

Note: You want to set this exercise up for success. This means you and your partner's mental and physical state should be calm and relaxed. Just be mindful that certain topics may lead to tension that can get in the way of listening but that can also be transformed through listening.

In fact, when discussing a charged or stressful topic, either you or your partner may get re-activated and start re-experiencing the symptoms of stress: the early physical, emotional, or cognitive warning signs (see Tool #7 Knowing Your Early Warning Signs). Even though this is a memory, just reflecting on the memory can lead to diffuse arousal with an elevated heartbeat, increased blood pressure, sweating, tensing, and other signs. If this starts to happen, it is important to stop for a moment, take the time to be silent, take a series of deep breaths, and wait until the arousal decreases. Return to Tool #8 and breathe into and through the strain. Then return to the topic if possible or select a less charged topic. It is very difficult to do reflective listening when either of you are overly charged.

TOOL #31

NUDGING Self

*Purpose:* To give yourself a well-timed, appropriate, and effective encouragement.

*Background:* It is possible that some of the previous tools provided can seem like a lot of work. It is also possible that you get started in a positive direction and your energy flags. The work of thriving may get a bit much or tiresome. It is also possible that you have tried different techniques and they are not working. Sometimes a simple nudge helps.

*Exercise:* Review the NUDGE model outlined here.

<u>N</u>otice something inside you, some aspect of your life that is incomplete. Alternately, it could be a yearning or striving for a higher state of happiness or consciousness. This could be an inkling, a tugging, an inner voice, a stirring. It could also be any of the signs discussed previously: early strain warning signs (physical, emotional, cognitive, social; see Tool #7) or later warning signs (see Tool #13).

<u>U</u>nderstand that you are completely responsible for doing something about it. This could be setting an intention, making a decision, taking some positive action, or doing any of the activities from this tool-kit.

<u>D</u>ecide what you need to do. Instead of procrastinating or weighing all the pros and cons, just decide to do it. Decide on one thing.

Use the following <u>G</u>uidelines. Read these guidelines as much as you need to.

<u>En</u>courage yourself in any or all of the following ways, always staying healthy as you proceed.

• Give yourself confidence • Review the C of confidence • Do something to hearten yourself • Cheer for yourself • Share positive belief in yourself with another • Inspire yourself through music, writing, dancing, watching a movie • Raise your spirits • Uplift • Motivate • Throw down a positive challenge to yourself • Use positive statements or affirmations • Use positive coping statements • Draw on your own self-efficacy • Walk the talk

## GUIDELINES FOR SELF-NUDGING

I AM GENTLE WITH MYSELF.

I AM DOING MY BEST.

I AM EXACTLY WHERE I NEED TO BE AND

I AM READY TO TAKE THE NEXT STEP IN MY LIFE.

HOWEVER SMALL OR LARGE, THAT NEXT STEP IS RIGHT FOR ME AT THIS TIME.

I RECOGNIZE EACH OF THE FOLLOWING PRINCIPLES

IN TERMS OF MY OWN EXPERIENCE.

THESE PRINCIPLES ARE ACTING NOW TO BRING ABOUT

POSITIVE CHANGE IN MY LIFE.

❖ I am designed to learn so much that I can place myself in stressful situations for the purpose of my growth and transformation.

❖ I can transform my approach to stress from "the kiss of death" to "the spice of life."

❖ I have an innate raw coping power; I can tap into this and work with stress as part of my own transformation.

❖ My values determine the level through which I process stress, from severe distress to a rich uplifting experience of thriving.

❖ My social groups can help me tap into my raw coping power and help me transform stress into an experience of thriving with others in my group.

❖ I show audacity in my quest for conversion, peak experiences, flourishing, or thriving.

❖ My nervous system is a well-oiled feedback system, allowing me to deal with stress at every stage.

# | 4 |

# This Is Your Nudge

THE INTRODUCTION TO THIS BOOK made reference to the inner witness that remains impervious to the stressors and strains of life. This idea comes from many spiritual traditions, which some say are as old as the dawn of civilization. I also shared many stories of resilience. Some of those date back hundreds and even thousands of years while some are occurring right now. It is clear that human beings have always known about their ability to take the good from even the most tragic events and use that good to strengthen their being, their lives, and their community.

Throughout the book I also made reference to research, modern science. This research also points to tools, techniques, and training that effectively arm individuals, workers, families, and organizations to deal with stress and thrive. Among this research are programs that help motivate people to change, to nudge them to explore and develop their own tools and resources that will help them move from distress to resilience and to thriving. This is described in the NUDGE tool (Tool #31 in the previous chapter). There are different ways to nudge. You can nudge yourself, as I suggest. Someone else can nudge you. Perhaps a person gave you this book as a gift was nudging? You can live in a community that has wonderful walking or bike paths and access to nature that invites you to exercise and enjoy fresh air. Or you can work in a company or agency that provides incentives to you for taking a stress management class.

However nudging is meant to happen, I hope that you have been sufficiently nudged by now. There is a part of you—call it that inner guardian—that wants you to do better and that wants you to relax and raise your level of happiness, your consciousness, and your setpoint. There are stories all around you: your own, from history, in books, in movies. Each of these is also nudging you. And they will always continue to do so.

I hope you remember that this nudging force and your inner witness are always there, rooting for you to move beyond just coping to thrive and flourish in your life ... with AUDACITY!

If you ever forget this, if you ever get bogged down in the negative coping cycle, in addiction, in distress, I hope you can turn back to the principles, the lenses, and the tools in this book and tap into your raw coping power. Perhaps something in here will spark you along into that deeper knowing. Go past the stressors, the strains, the negative habits and into the borders of your life. At the end of the day, I hope you are ever nudged inward to awaken what you already know to be true.

I am convinced:
> to fathom the silence
> the body must confess many
> tight secrets

I am convinced:
> to dwell in the angerless place
> we need but empty our hearts
> but for the joy we were born with

I am convinced, now, with certainty:
> that these things are possible;
> that you were born to fathom,
> and dwell in, joy

But these are words,
> issuing like tumbleweed across
> the desert
> now here and gone

Go, start now:
> your restlessness craves taming
> your wounds await the healing sun

and in a moment...
> a happy lapse in your sleeplessness
> you will arrive home

# | A |

# APPENDIX

CORPORATE ASSESSMENT TOOLS

- ORGANIZATIONAL (SYSTEM) STRESS AUDIT

- CULTURE OF RESILIENCE

On the following pages, readers will find two tools that can be used by human resource professionals or those who advise and support organizational-level strategies for stress management. This includes professionals in organizational development, occupational health, organizational psychologists, and providers of employee assistance services.

Please use these tools as needed. The author asks that credit be given whenever these tools are utilized.

## ORGANIZATIONAL (SYSTEM) STRESS AUDIT

*Background.* Principle 2 in *Raw Coping Power* states: *We can systematically transform our entire approach to stress.* Key ideas in that principle are conveyed in the words *systematic* and *entire.* The discussion of this principle clearly states that systemic approaches are the most scientifically valid approaches to workplace stress. They integrate strategies to enhance three areas: work environment and production flow, communication, and individual coping skills. Improvements in the *shared* work environment are much more effective when they are combined with psycho-educational programs for employees. And stress management courses for employees are more effective when combined with improved communication and work flow.

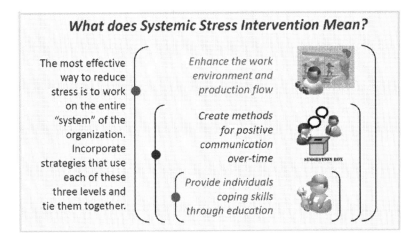

**What does Systemic Stress Intervention Mean?**

The most effective way to reduce stress is to work on the entire "system" of the organization. Incorporate strategies that use each of these three levels and tie them together.

*Enhance the work environment and production flow*

*Create methods for positive communication over-time*

*Provide individuals coping skills through education*

The following check-list is provided to help assess whether or not your organization has features in place that can promote a more pro-active rather than reactive approach to stress. Most importantly, when using this check-list it is critical to involve and engage workers at all levels, especially from staff who are most "in the trenches" and most exposed to highly demanding work situations.

## ORGANIZATIONAL (SYSTEM) STRESS AUDIT

This check-list is best used within a committee or task-force comprised of workers from all job-levels and representing different job areas. Note that there are five primary domains (Assessment, Communication, Work Stressors, Health Promotion, and Individual Education). A systemic approach shows (a) strength in all five areas, and (b) integration across areas. See "Integration Questions" below.

### I. Assessments (typically done in early stages of systemic intervention)

- ☐ Ergonomic analysis of the work space (how work is conducted, mechanics, physical environment and constraints)
- ☐ Health risk or wellness appraisals that are used to plan programs
- ☐ Work communication assessments that are used to plan programs
- ☐ Perceptions of work stress and work climate that are used in planning
- ☐ Individual assessments of role stressors that are used to plan programs
- ☐ Use established stress analyses (job strain, effort-reward imbalance)
- ☐ Other:

### II. Improvements in Communication

- ☐ Clarify lines of reporting
- ☐ Clear action steps in every meeting
- ☐ Processes for improving clarity of communication
- ☐ Significant staff-management coordination (Participative Management)
- ☐ Commitment to improvements through efficient committees
- ☐ Training for managers in effective (heart-centered) leadership
- ☐ On-going steering, advisory, or wellness committee whose suggestions are seriously reviewed and acted upon by management
- ☐ Use of focus groups to ascertain employee perceptions of stress
- ☐ Anonymous (suggestion boxes) requests for pointers on stress reduction
- ☐ Regular opportunities for management-employee interaction
- ☐ Opportunities for managers to clarify their roles and responsibilities
- ☐ Employee ownership
- ☐ Other:

### III. Modification of Work Stressors

- ☐ Increased work control for employees
- ☐ Self-managed work teams
- ☐ Flexible work schedules
- ☐ Review and Modification of workloads
- ☐ Job rotation
- ☐ Opportunities for work breaks (e.g., stretch periods)
- ☐ Enhanced performance appraisals that empower
- ☐ Planned changes in production work flows and mechanics
- ☐ Environmental quality reviews (air quality/hazard exposure)
- ☐ Other:

## ORGANIZATIONAL (SYSTEM) STRESS AUDIT (CONTINUED)

| IV. Improvements in Health Promotion |
|---|
| ☐ Opportunities for workers to be physically active during the work day |
| ☐ Group-related wellness activities and challenges |
| ☐ Wellness is part of work culture (sports, competitions, challenges) |
| ☐ Providing access to yoga, tai chi, or qigong classes |
| ☐ Promotion of EAP as an integral part of wellness |
| ☐ Other: |

| V. Individual-level Resources and Changes |
|---|
| ☐ Education on cognitive-behavioral strategies for stress include: |
|    o   identifying workplace stressors |
|    o   discussing strategies for dealing with the stressors |
|    o   promote innovative ways of coping |
|    o   developing action plans for coping |
|    o   realistic appraisal of those plans |
|    o   follow-up and revision to improve |
| ☐ Access to coaching for job-crafting |
| ☐ Programs that promote and de-stigmatize use of EAP or other benefits |
| ☐ Other techniques that reduce arousal are beneficial as well such as mindfulness, meditation, or training in relaxation response. |
| ☐ Other: |

Some Integration Questions

☐ Do assessments in the first area help determine priorities in the other areas (communication, modify work stressors, improve health promotion, and enhance individual-level resource)?

☐ Do communication strategies help to promote and de-stigmatize the use of health promotion and individual-level education?

☐ Are attempts to reduce work stressors only top-down and administrative or do they integrate staff-level input (communication)?

☐ Have you found ways to efficiently tie health promotion and work stressor strategies together so that workers see that the burden of stress management is not entirely on them?

## CULTURE OF RESILIENCE

*Background.* In any work setting, resilience may be viewed both as recovery from previous adverse events as well as a preparedness for future adverse events. Resilience has preparedness aspects in that resilient organizations learn from (and are capable of learning from) future adversity. These dual capacities to recover and prepare are greater when an organization has developed the *Five Competencies of Resilience* (see Lens #5 and Tool #26). In addition to these *Five Cs*, organizations demonstrate healthy leadership. Together, Five Cs and healthy leadership make up the *Core* of resilience.

This tool identifies eight different types of challenges or areas of adversity: significant change, crisis, strain, growth, and problems in the areas of health, safety, personal/behavioral issues, and financial. Each of these may have occurred in the recent past, entailing recovery; or each may occur in the future, requiring preparedness.

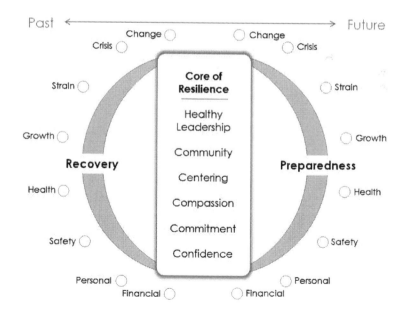

*Step 1. Your Resilience Core.* Assess six core competencies that allow the company to (1) re-establish strength following recent hardship and adversity, and (2) learn from previous problems as a way to be prepared for future hardships.

INSTRUCTIONS. For each item below, indicate how often you see evidence that the competency exists in your work area, department, or organization as a whole.

| | Rarely | Little | Some | Often | Always |
|---|---|---|---|---|---|
| **Healthy Leadership.** We have effective business leaders and managers. They set the vision, develop business plans and structures, show care for employees and model resilience. | 1 | 2 | 3 | 4 | 5 |
| **Community.** We make efforts to work together, building community, inclusiveness, honoring diversity, and receiving from and contributing to the surrounding community where we work. | 1 | 2 | 3 | 4 | 5 |
| **Centering.** We make efforts to work at an even pace, structure work in ways that respect human limits and energy, and provide quality resources to help workers with stress-related problems. | 1 | 2 | 3 | 4 | 5 |
| **Compassion.** At all levels, from top management to daily interactions with internal and external customers, people are treated with respect and concern for well-being. Human resource benefits follow values of compassion and care. | 1 | 2 | 3 | 4 | 5 |
| **Commitment.** Employees are engaged, present, and committed to doing high quality work. They persist in the face of troubles to solve problems. | 1 | 2 | 3 | 4 | 5 |
| **Confidence.** Employees show strength and positivity in their attitude toward work and life. We help build confidence in each other as our business/mission makes a great contribution to others/society. | 1 | 2 | 3 | 4 | 5 |
| TOTAL SCORE HERE ➜ | | | | | |

*Step 2. Your Response to Recent Adversity.* Assess eight areas where your organization (or department) recently faced problems.

RECOVERY--Previous/current adversity. How well has your organization (department) recovered from or is currently responding to the 8 challenges listed below? Use this '0' to '5' point scale to make your rating.

| | |
|---|---|
| 0 = Does not apply (did not happen) | 3 = Moderately, we are just coping |
| 1 = Not very well, problems still exist | 4 = Well, we are healthy |
| 2 = Not Well, risks are still there | 5 = Very Well, we are stronger now |

| | |
|---|---|
| 1. *Change.* A significant change or serious, major conflict inside the company | ⓪ ① ② ③ ④ ⑤ |
| 2. *Crisis.* A critical event, catastrophe, or crisis we did not foresee | ⓪ ① ② ③ ④ ⑤ |
| 3. *Strain.* Staff endured strain at work (more demands; job insecurity; unclear direction; harassment; bullying) | ⓪ ① ② ③ ④ ⑤ |
| 4. *Growth.* We struggled adapting to pressures (internal, external, market), growth, or downsizing | ⓪ ① ② ③ ④ ⑤ |
| 5. *Health.* Increase or major health challenges (e.g., claims data, reduced wellness scores or lack of engagement, absenteeism) | ⓪ ① ② ③ ④ ⑤ |
| 6. *Safety.* Increase in safety issues and/or accidents | ⓪ ① ② ③ ④ ⑤ |
| 7. *Personal.* Increase in or many employees struggling with life transitions (newly married, new parent, divorce, empty nest, caring for older parent, etc.) | ⓪ ① ② ③ ④ ⑤ |
| 8. *Financial.* Employee financial pressures. | ⓪ ① ② ③ ④ ⑤ |

TOTAL SCORE HERE ➔

*Step 3. Your Preparedness for Future Adversity.* Assess eight areas where your organization (or department) might face future problems.

PREPAREDNESS--*Future Risk.* How prepared is your organization (department) to deal with the 8 challenges should they occur soon?

| 0= Does not apply (will not happen) | 3 = Moderately, we would just get by |
|---|---|
| 1= Not very well, we would succumb | 4 = Well, we can handle it |
| 2= Not Well, there would be costs | 5 = Very Well, we would grow from it |

| | 0 | 1 | 2 | 3 | 4 | 5 |
|---|---|---|---|---|---|---|
| 1. *Change.* A significant change or serious, major conflict inside the company | ⓪ | ① | ② | ③ | ④ | ⑤ |
| 2. *Crisis.* A critical event, catastrophe, or crisis we may not foresee | ⓪ | ① | ② | ③ | ④ | ⑤ |
| 3. *Strain.* Staff endures strain at work (more demands; job insecurity; unclear direction; harassment; bullying) | ⓪ | ① | ② | ③ | ④ | ⑤ |
| 4. *Growth.* We struggle adapting to pressures (internal, external, market), growth, or downsizing | ⓪ | ① | ② | ③ | ④ | ⑤ |
| 5. *Health.* Increase or major health challenges (e.g., claims data, reduced wellness scores or lack of engagement, absenteeism) | ⓪ | ① | ② | ③ | ④ | ⑤ |
| 6. *Safety.* Increase in safety issues and/or accidents | ⓪ | ① | ② | ③ | ④ | ⑤ |
| 7. *Personal.* Increase in, or many employees struggling with, life transitions (newly married, new parent, divorce, empty nest, caring for older parent, etc.) | ⓪ | ① | ② | ③ | ④ | ⑤ |
| 8. *Financial.* Employee financial pressures. | ⓪ | ① | ② | ③ | ④ | ⑤ |

TOTAL SCORE HERE ➔

SCORING AND APPLICATION

Resilience Core scores can range from 6 to 30. Scores greater than 23 suggest high levels of resilience and scores less than 15 suggest need for improvement. Either way, pay attention to specific areas with lower scores.

Your total Recovery and Preparedness scores can range from 0 to 40. Total scores greater than 30 suggest high levels of recovery or preparedness, whereas scores less than 20 suggest the need to attend high-risk areas.

Providing workers with tools in this book can be helpful. However, for low recovery scores we strongly recommend using an employee assistance (EAP) resource, especially after critical incidents. Similarly, low preparedness scores should be reviewed with your EAP and any other resources that can help (organizational development, safety, etc.).

# Definitions

**Adaptation.** To adjust or make suitable for the specific end of growth and
learning, to productively learn from a situation in ways that allow us to
interact positively with that situation in the future. In *Raw Coping Power*,
adaptation is one part of the four-part definition of stress as described in
Principle #1. By this definition, the experience of adaptation is always a
potential outcome from any encounter with stress or strain.

**Addiction.** In *Raw Coping Power*, I make the distinction between a formal
addiction and an addictive tendency. Formally, an addiction refers to an
ingrained or compulsive attachment to a substance (such as alcohol,
drugs, or tobacco) or a process (such as emotions, adrenaline,
relationships, sex, gambling, or Internet). An addiction usually begins
when an individual forms a psychological and neurochemical association
between the substance or process and an increase in pleasure and/or a
reduction in felt pain or tension. An addictive tendency refers to a way of
coping with stress in which the individual is more likely to choose
expedient and ultimately ineffective methods (to reduce tension) than
more planned approaches that actually address the stressor and strain

and lead to better health. The *Diagnostic and Statistical Manual of Mental Disorders*, Fourth Edition(DSM-IV) prefers the term *dependence* instead of *addiction* and defines dependence when there are three or more of seven criteria. The DSM-IV applies these criteria to drugs but we extend it to all substances and other processes. (1) Tolerance: There is an increased need for the substance/process over time to get the same effect; (2) Withdrawal symptoms: The user experiences withdrawal symptoms when he or she does not use the substance/process; (3) Continued use of substance/process despite harm; (4) Loss of control; (5) Attempts to cut down are unsuccessful; (6) Salience: Significant time is spent obtaining or thinking about the substance/process; and (7) Reduced involvement: The user has given up or reduced his or her involvement in social, occupational or recreational activities due to the substance/process.

**Audacity.** Audacity is often defined as the willingness to take bold risks, usually in ways that go against social expectations. In *Raw Coping Power*, audacity refers to a particular zest and vigor to fully welcome, work through, and overcome stress and adversity as a positive challenge. This goes beyond willingness to actual expression of raw coping power in behavior. Audacity may be seen as a super-thriving attitude. Examples of phrases associated with audacity are "Bring it on!" or "Let's do this!" The audacious person, seeing the potential growth and success within the stressor rather than the potential danger and set-backs, takes decisive action to transform the stressor into a positive outcome.

**Conversion.** A conversion experience is often defined as a positive and enlightening religious or mystical experience in which the mental framework, attitude, beliefs, and identity of the individual are permanently altered. Religious conversion typically refers to the awakening of religious knowledge or understanding within a human being who had previously no belief in or concern with religious or spiritual matters. Examples of phrases associated with conversion are "I have seen the light!" or "I am not the person I used to be." In *Raw Coping Power*, conversion is one of several types of positive experiences that can result from stress (see Principle #7). However, adversity is not a necessary condition for conversion. The religious and mystical literature is replete with many examples of saints and mystics who experienced enlightenment because of stress and adversity.

**Coping Style.** In the scientific literature, coping styles often refer to the ways people make efforts to reduce demands and stressors but without concern as to whether those efforts are effective. Like any "style" it refers to the manner or way we design our approach. Among the many categories of different types of styles, there is general agreement that approaches that avoid, escape, or neglect the stressor are less effective, especially if these are habitual. More effective styles include problem solving, cognitive hardiness, activating a healthy lifestyle, seeking social support, consulting with advisors, spiritual practices, for examples. In *Raw Coping Power*, coping style is a key component of the Stress > Evaluate > Cope framework. Tool #17 Review Your Coping Style Factors provides a survey for personal review.

**Efficacy.** Refers to a sense of confidence that one can have an influence on, rather than being only a passive responder to events and situations. Individuals with self-efficacy have the power to produce desired effects and see themselves as effective.

**Flourish.** To grow well and experience a period of success, productivity, abundance, or excellence, especially with a sense of continuous growth. A sustained experience of cycles of increased functioning beyond a level of healthy coping, where new challenges result in increases in functioning. In *Raw Coping Power*, flourishing is one of several types of positive experiences that can result from stress (see Principle #7). However, adversity is not a necessary condition for flourishing to occur. Importantly, people can have disabilities and not only flourish in their lives but the disability itself becomes the stimulus for such flourishing.

**Inner Guardian.** A metaphor for mental and emotional processes that help us to calmly observe events, choose mindful and skillful responses, and protect our mind and body from receiving a negative effect as a result of events, stressors, or our response to such events or stressors.

**Job Crafting.** A specific set of tools whereby employees reimagine or redesign their jobs in personal ways that they find meaningful. Tool #25 guides readers in a job crafting exercise.

**Lifestyle.** Generally, the typical way that an individual leads life or carries out the routines of living. Healthy lifestyle, a major subject in *Raw Coping Power*, refers to routines of diet, exercise, energy management, and sleep. It is commonly believed—and research supports this—that maintaining physical and mental health increases our biological longevity. The more time we spend on physical fitness and good diet, the healthier lifestyle we may have. In *Raw Coping Power*, lifestyle is a key component of the Stress > Evaluate > Cope framework and Tool #16 provides a self-assessment exercise.

**Peak Experience.** The psychologist Abraham Maslow described a peak experience as a state of witnessing or cognitive blissfulness. Other definitions include a sense of extraordinariness, ecstasy, high levels of joy, deep appreciation of beauty, a sense of awe at life, sudden insight into meaning of life, interconnectedness, harmony, and euphoria. In *Raw Coping Power*, a peak experience is one of several types of positive experiences that can result from stress (see Principle #7). However, adversity is not a necessary condition for a peak experience to occur.

**Potentiation.** To bring out the positive and life-supporting potential of something. Lens #4 is devoted to this concept as it applies to stress. Namely, that stress holds the potential for positive outcomes, including resilience, thriving, and flourishing. The concept of potentiation is seen in medicine as the enhancement of one agent by another so that the combined effect is greater than the sum of the effects of each one alone. As applied here, the two agents are stress and our raw coping power. This means that stress or adversity (as one agent) can create a greater positive effect when combined with our raw coping power than if either of the two (stress and coping) operated alone.

**Resilience.** The ability to recover from adversity, bounce back to a normal or high level of functioning, and also learn from having gone through the experience of adversity. In *Raw Coping Power*, resilience is one of several types of experiences that can result from stress (see Principle #7). It is helpful to compare resilience with these other experiences (flourishing, thriving, peak experiences, and conversion). Each of the latter may occur whether or not there is a preceding stressor or adversity. In contrast, adversity is a necessary condition for the process of resilience to occur. Tapping into this experience is a key part of the message in this book, which is why the very first Tool (#1) asks readers to recall, journal and possibly share personal stories of resilience.

**Set-Point.** There are different definitions of this term in reference to weight control and obesity and also in reference to happiness. A happiness set-point refers to a fixed range of happiness that we tend to return to throughout our life following either positive or very positive experiences as well as negative or even very negative experiences. Claims are made that our well-being set-point is approximately 50 percent genetic and 50 percent learned. In *Raw Coping Power* set-point pertains to the *general* level of functioning that includes happiness as well as health, consciousness, and the ability to function effectively in all areas of life: social, community, financial, family, and career. We extend the meaning of the term *set* to refer to our settled ways of doing things (fixed routines and habits) as well as to what we "settle" for in the idiomatic use of that term. That is, our willingness to stomach, put up with, or tolerate (see Tolerance/Tolerating definition). So our set-point refers to that fixed range but also to the habits and tolerance attitudes that either keep us in that fixed range or raise our overall level.

**Strain.** The experience of exertion, the taxing of one's energy and abilities, or reaching a limit in energy or ability, often in response to harm or perceived harm. Strain is often the result of (a) a stressful event (see "stressor"), (b) a way of thinking about or responding to a stressful event, or (c) internal thinking patterns and habits—one's own internal "chatter." The latter definition indicates that individuals can create their own strain, without an outside stressor. This occurs through obsessing about past or future events. In this book, strain is one part of the four-part definition of stress as described in Principle #1. By this definition, the experience of strain by itself does not constitute an experience of stress and yet strain is often the cause of stress.

**Stress.** In *Raw Coping Power*, stress consists of four interrelated parts, as described in Principle #1. These are responding, stressor, strain, and adaptation. Taken together, we define stress as "the experience of responding to harm or potential harm or stressors that can tax your ability to cope, producing tension or strain and/or lead to productive learning or adaptation." There are three key points to note about this definition. First, it indicates that how we respond to harm (real or perceived) can produce tension or learning or both. This means that how we respond to harm does not necessarily have to lead to tension and yet there may still be some experience of stress. Second, stress is defined by our response to the harm, which may or may not include strain but always does include the *potential* for strain. Third, every response to harm can help us manage or transform the environment where the harm exists (see Adaptation) and has the potential to teach us something (see Potentiation).

**Stressor.** An initial stimulus, situation, or event that places a demand on our energy, attention, or other capacity and usually involves a harm or threat or the perception of harm or threat. In *Raw Coping Power*, a stressor is one part of the four-part definition of stress as described in Principle #1. By this definition, a stressor by itself does not constitute an experience of stress and may or may not actually result in stress. Stressors occur in many different life domains. Four common domains include relationships, career, finances, and health.

**Thrive.** To thrive means to grow strongly or vigorously, to be successful, or to prosper. When we thrive we either develop new strengths or tap into hidden strengths. In *Raw Coping Power*, thriving is one of several types of positive experiences that can result from stress (see Principle #7). Adversity is not a necessary condition for thriving to occur. However, thriving occurs when adversity leads to an increase in functioning or performance after the exposure to adversity. Our consciousness and sense of aliveness is greater after the stress than before the stress. Thriving may often be activated when there is a change in environment or a change in the situation of one's life. Some of us are more likely to thrive in one type of environment or with certain types of conditions where the pattern or timing of stressors helps us to learn and grow.

**Tolerance/Tolerating.** In this book, tolerance has a specific meaning and pertains to the tendency to endure, put up with, allow, or stomach stressors or strains without responding in ways that seek to address those stressors or strains. Tolerance is on one end of a continuum, and intentional responding is on the other end. Our chances of experiencing strain increase the longer we tolerate a stressor, especially for too long a period of time. Our chances of addressing the stressor and reducing the strain increase the sooner we effectively respond. Individuals tolerate different things to different degrees, and individuals vary in how much any particular stressor is tolerable. It is assumed that individuals always have a choice as to whether they will tolerate a stressor or seek avenues to address the stressor.

**Transformation.** To change the state of something often in a marked or notable way. The concept of transformation (from stress-to-thriving) is central to the idea of raw coping power because such power has, by its nature, the ability to modify potentially harmful situations into opportunities for growth. Principle #2 describes transforming stress from being "the kiss of death" to "the spice of life." This means that the stressor or strain in themselves are not necessarily changed, but how we respond to them—our whole attitude toward stress—has changed so that we meet the situation with hope, optimism, efficacy, and resilience.

**Uplifts.** Any event that we experience that enhances our mood creates a sense of well-being or happiness. Many different types of events can range from feeling joy from receiving affection, relief at hearing good news, the pleasure of a good night's rest, seeing a plant grow, watching the sun filter through the window, to seeing one's pet at the end of the day. We know something is an uplift when it leads you to feel well, hopeful, optimistic, effective, or resilient. Uplifts may be seen as the opposite of a stressor. As such, any event or situation that has the potential for producing an increase in well-being or happiness may be said to be an uplift.

**Values.** A standard or a principle that one considers worthwhile or worth pursuing or upholding in word, behavior, and lifestyle. This standard is often what individuals consider to be most important in life or that has the most meaning or the greatest potential to help us create a meaningful life. In *Raw Coping Power*, values can influence the level we process stress (Principle #4) from distress to thriving. Values also predispose us to see the potential of stress as an opportunity for growth (Lens #4). Values are explored in Tool #6 with examples including family, beauty, spirituality, security, and self-direction.

# Resources

THE LIST OF RESOURCES IN THIS SECTION IS NOT EXHAUSTIVE. My intention is to help you see that there is truly an abundance of resources available for dealing with all aspects of stress and to give you enough tools and insights to get you started. Also, many resources can be found in the Tools section.

The Internet, including many free instructional videos on YouTube, may also provide you with tools that complement or reinforce your healthy lifestyle. For easy search, Internet sites are marked with a symbol ✦.

Please visit our website at www.rawcopingpower.com for free downloadable resources as well, including an extensively documented Notes section for this book.

**Original sources on the idea that many people are living "asleep" or in a relatively unconscious state.** *Raw Coping Power* assumes that human beings have far more potential than they realize or give themselves credit for. To be clear, this is not the same as the urban myth which states that humans only use some small percentage of their brains. There is no scientific evidence to support that myth. In contrast, the sources here come more from the field of philosophy, human development, and transpersonal psychology. They are provided to readers who wish to further advance their knowledge and the potential of their internal, self-remembering, conscious observer or witness.

Gurdjieff, G.I. (2012). *In Search of Being: The Fourth Way of Consciousness.* New York: Fourth Way Editions.

Ouspensky, P.D. (1981). *The Psychology of Man's Possible Evolution*. New York: Random House.

Wilber, K. (2004). *The Simple Feeling of Being: Embracing Your True Nature*. Boston and London: Shambhala.

Tart, C. T. (2001). *Waking Up: Overcoming the Obstacles to Human Potential*. Lincoln, Neb.: New Science Library.

Almaas, A.H. (2000). *Elements of the Real in Man (Diamond Heart, Book 1)*. Boston and London: Shambhala.

Hawkins, D.R. (2012). *Power vs. Force: The Hidden Determinants of Human Behavior* (revised edition). Carlsbad, Calif.: Hay House.

**Self-help books on the concept of set-point that help you tap into your raw coping power.** Dozens of self-help books help readers understand their own self-limiting beliefs and behaviors. These popular books come at the idea of "setting your sights higher" from somewhat different angles, and I suggest you preview them before selecting one that might be right for you. Each one can work depending upon a right fit.

Fritz, R. (1989). *The Path of Least Resistance: Learning to Become the Creative Force in Your Own Life*. New York: Fawcett.
+ Related website: www.robertfritz.com.

Hendricks, G. (2009). *The Big Leap*. New York: Harper Collins.
+ Related website: www.hendricks.com.

Shimoff, M. (2008). *Happy for No Reason*. New York: Free Press.
+ Related website: www.happyfornoreason.com.

Nichols, L. (2009). *No Matter What*. New York: Wellness Central/Hachette.
+ Related website: www.motivatingthemasses.com.

McGraw, P. (2001). *Self Matters: Creating Your Life from the Inside Out*. New York: Free Press.
+ Related website: www.drphil.com/articles/category/6/ (see Self Matters).

Hanson, R. (2013). *Hardwiring Happiness: The New Brain Science of Contentment, Calm, and Confidence*. New York: Crown.
+ Related website: www.rickhanson.net.

**Tool #2 encourages you to adapt a daily mind-body practice.** Here are some books and resources that I have found particularly helpful. Ultimately, you have to find and stick to your own daily routine. This could be 15 minutes to

120 minutes and include any one or a mixture of different practices including Qigong, yoga, meditation, visualizations, relaxation, inspirational reading, or prayer. I encourage you to incorporate at least one of the other thirty *Raw Coping Power* tools into this routine.

Jahnke, R.O. (1998). *The Healer Within: Using Traditional Chinese Techniques to Release Your Body's Own Medicine, Movement, Massage, Meditation, Breathing.* San Francisco: HarperCollins.

✦ Related website: www.healerwithin.com.

Luskin, F., & Pelletier, K. (2005). *Stress Free for Good: 10 Scientifically Proven Life Skills for Health and Happiness.* New York: HarperCollins.

Pelletier, K.R. (2000). *The Best Alternative Medicine: What Works? What Does Not?* New York: Fireside/Simon and Schuster.

✦ Related website: www.drpelletier.com.

Eden, D. (2008). *Energy Medicine: Balancing Your Body's Energies for Optimal Health, Joy, and Vitality.* New York: Penguin.

✦ Related website: www.innersource.net/innersource.

Goldstein, J. (2013). *Mindfulness: A Practical Guide to Awakening.* Louisville, Colorado: Sounds True.

✦ Related websites: www.dharma.org and www.soundstrue.com (shop for Mindfulness).

Wordsworth, C.F., & Glanville, G.N. (2007). *Quantum Change Made Easy: Breakthroughs in Personal Transformation, Self-Healing and Achieving the Best of Who You Are.* Scottsdale, Ariz.: Resonance Publishing.

✦ Related website: www.resonancerepatterning.net.

Kabat-Zinn, J. (2013). *Full Catastrophe Living.* New York: Bantam/Random House.

✦ Related website: www.mindfulnesscds.com.

**Recommended simple relaxations and meditations.** Here are a diverse selection of YouTube videos that teach autogenic training, deep breathing, and other meditative practices:

| Practice | YouTube |
| --- | --- |
| Sitting Qigong with Dr. Roger Jahnke | www.youtube.com/watch?v=dWvICLbjVJo |
| Progressive Muscle Relaxation Exercise | www.youtube.com/watch?v=HFwCKKa--18 |
| Cosmic Journey Guided Meditation | www.youtube.com/watch?v=AWxGQOZSbxk |
| Guided Meditation with Deepak Chopra | www.youtube.com/watch?v=kWe501bBel8 |
| Simple Meditation with Kris Carr | www.youtube.com/watch?v=sy8q3E6nJ-l |
| Feelingization with Arielle Ford | www.youtube.com/watch?v=ucJBNWGSk8A |
| Body Meditation with Jack Kornfield | www.youtube.com/watch?v=COBSzdqDvAk |
| Guided Loving Kindness Meditation with Sharon Salzburg | www.youtube.com/watch?v=W3uLqt69Vyl |
| Morning Meditation with Carolyn Myss | www.youtube.com/watch?v=B5sJQHCe-1s |
| Compassion (Tong Lin) Meditation with Pema Chodron | www.youtube.com/watch?v=QwqlurCvXuM |
| Guided Meditation with Eckhart Tolle | www.youtube.com/watch?v=1sQ0DTF2tAM |
| Guided Meditation with John Kabat-Zinn | www.youtube.com/watch?v=aS5QpPRFdbg |
| Autogenic Relaxation for Pain Relief | www.youtube.com/watch?v=aKo8vQDa4wY |
| Autogenic Relaxation | www.youtube.com/watch?v=m0e8l8dUxuA |
| Special Tree Guided Meditation | www.youtube.com/watch?v=C9bZkCNnppM |

*These exercises are not intended as a substitute for medical advice. Consult a physician if you feel ongoing distress. Make sure to avoid operating machinery or driving a vehicle while doing or following these exercises. This list of exercises is not meant to convey an endorsement of these programs or persons.

**Helpful books on healthy living and developing a healthy lifestyle.** In addition to daily mind-body practice, there is no substitute for a healthy diet, regular exercise, and good use of rest, relaxation, and sufficient sleep. These books each address healthy lifestyle in a different way. Again, preview these before selecting one. Any of them can work depending on the right fit.

Katz, D.L. (2013). *Disease-Proof: The Remarkable Truth about What Makes Us Well.* New York: Hudson Street/Penguin.

  ✛ Related website: www.davidkatzmd.com.

Mayo Clinic. (2012). *Mayo Clinic Healthy Heart for Life.* New York: Time Home Entertainment.

  ✛ Related website: www.mayoclinic.org/healthy-lifestyle.

Carr, K. (2007). *Crazy Sexy Cancer Tips.* Guilford, Conn.: Morris Publishing.

  ✛ Related website: http://kriscarr.com.

Oz, M., & Roizen, M.F. (2009). *YOU: The Owner's Manual*. New York: Harper Collins.
  ✦ Related website: www.doctoroz.com.
Weil, A. (2008). *8 Weeks to Optimum Health: A Proven Program for Taking Full Advantage of Your Body's Natural Healing Power*. New York: Knopf.
  ✦ Related website: www.drweil.com.
Aldana, S. (2008). *The Culprit and The Cure: Why Lifestyle Is the Culprit behind America's Poor Health*. Mapleton, Utah: Maple Mountain.
  ✦ Related website: www.stevealdana.com.
Clement, B.R. (2007). *Hippocrates Life Force: Superior Health and Longevity*. Summertown, TN: Healthy Living.
  ✦ Related website: http://hippocratesinst.org.

In addition to these books, there are two magazines that I recommend. Both have online resources that are frequently updated.
  ✦ Visit *Experience Life* at http://experiencelife.com where you can also get a subscription.
  ✦ Visit *Spirituality & Health* at http://spiritualityhealth.com/ where you can also get a subscription.

**More books on resilience: What is it with "bouncing"?** If you are interested in a deeper dive into studying resilience, here are some additional books, all with the word *bounce* in their titles. And this list of books is not exhaustive. In the span of five years, it is not coincidental that so many have written on this subject. Many people in societies around the world are beginning to frame trauma and adversity in a new way. This is partly due to recent exposure to horrific events such war, hurricanes, tsunamis, acts of terrorism, revolutions, and steep financial downturns.

Salmansohn, K. (2007). *The Bounce Back Book: How to Thrive in the Face of Adversity, Setbacks, and Losses*. New York: Workman.
Moltz, B.J. (2008). *Bounce! Failure, Resiliency, and Confidence to Achieve Your Next Great Success*. Hoboken: Wiley.
McFarland, K. (2009). *Bounce: The Art of Turning Tough Times into Triumph*. New York: Crown Business.
Wicks, R. (2010). *Bounce: Living the Resilient Life*. New York: Oxford University Press.

Syed, M. (2010). *Bounce: Mozart, Federer, Picasso, Beckham, and the Science of Success.* New York: Harper.

Cawthorn, S. (2013). *Bounce Forward: How to Transform Crisis into Success.* Melbourne: Wiley.

**For a more technical review of resilience** from an organizational perspective, I recommend:

National Research Council. *A Ready and Resilient Workforce for the Department of Homeland Security: Protecting America's Front Line.* Washington, DC: The National Academies Press, 2013. (available from Institute of Medicine, http://www.iom.edu/, released September, 2013).

**Other helpful books on stress with tools and exercises.** On Amazon there are over 5,000 books and CDs in the category Self-Help: Stress Management. So it may be difficult to find just the right tool for you. This is just a brief list of some resources I am familiar with that might supplement your *Raw Coping Power* tool-kit.

Benson, H. (1975). *The Relaxation Response.* New York: HarperTorch.

Cunningham, J.B. (1997). *The Stress Management Sourcebook.* Los Angeles: Lowell House.

Sood, A. (2013). *The Mayo Clinic Guide to Stress-Free Living.* Boston: Da Capo Press.

Davis, M., Eshelman, E., & McKay, M. (2009). *The Relaxation and Stress Reduction Workbook* (New Harbinger Self-Help Workbook). Oakland, Calif.: New Harbinger.

Seaward, B.L. (2009). *Managing Stress: Principles and Strategies for Health and Well-being.* Boston: Jones & Bartlett.

Rossman, M.L. (2010). *The Worry Solution: Using Breakthrough Brain Science to Turn Stress and Anxiety into Confidence and Happiness.* New York: Three Rivers Press.

## Some Helpful Relaxation and Self-Help Audio CDs

Mark Grant, especially his Audio CDs *Calm and Confident* and *Overcoming Pain* ✛ http://overcomingpain.com.

Belleruth Naparstek has many self-guided imagery CDs that deal with a
variety of stress-related problems
+ http://belleruthnaparstek.com or www.healthjourneys.com.

**Some Online Resources for Stress**

The National Center for Complementary and Alternative Medicine is a
center of the National Institutes of Health. Look here for updates on the
latest research associated with alternative approaches to stress
reduction: + http://nccam.nih.gov/health/stress.

WebMD is a resource financed by advertising, third-party contributions and
sponsorships and has millions of page views per month. This particular
page: + www.webmd.com/balance/stress-management/default.htm.
Stress Stop offers a complete library of stress management resources,
specializing in common sense training materials for employees and
patients: + www.stressstop.com.
Gaiam and Gaiam TV provides information, goods and services to
customers who value the environment, a sustainable economy, healthy
lifestyles, alternative healthcare and personal development. The links
provided deal specifically with resources on stress:
+ www.gaiam.com/stress-relief and www.gaiamtv.com/search/gss/stress.

**Many resources promote an intentional way of viewing movies for the
purpose of stimulating personal growth.** One resource is the continually
updated film list from the website + www.spiritualityandpractice.com. This
site lists over thirty different spiritual practice categories from A to Z. This
includes Awareness, Compassion, Connections, Gratitude, Meaning,
Questing, Silence, Transformation, Wonder, Yearning, and Zeal.

The website authors, Frederic and Mary Ann Brussat, give instruction on
spiritual literacy or how to read the deeper meaning in a text or movie to
enhance meaning in our life. For example, let's take the practice of
transformation, which applies to our ability to use raw coping power to
transform stress. The Brussats suggest the theme of transformation can be
found in movies as diverse as the four listed here.

*Gravity* (2013). A medical engineer and an astronaut work together to survive after an accident leaves them adrift in space.

*Precious: Based on the Novel* Push *by Sapphire* (2009). In New York City's Harlem circa 1987, an overweight, abused, illiterate teen who is pregnant with her second child is invited to enroll in an alternative school in hopes that her life can head in a new direction.

*Regarding Henry* (1991). Henry is a lawyer who survives a shooting only to find he cannot remember anything. If that weren't enough, Henry also has to recover his speech and mobility, in a life he no longer fits into.

*Born on the Fourth of July* (1989). The biography of Ron Kovic. Paralyzed in the Vietnam War, he becomes an antiwar and pro-human rights political activist after feeling betrayed by the country he fought for.

Of course, this is just a brief sample and one movie may touch one person differently than it touches another. In just these four movies alone, we can find many of the principles and lenses at work in the stress-to-thriving transformation of the story characters.

Another helpful resource is the book *Taming Your Dragons: Making Peace with Your Emotions* by Sue-Anne MacGregor and David Barnes (2013). They integrate summaries about seventy movies into important lessons on working with emotional states. For example, they talk about *The Proposal* (2009). A pushy boss forces her young assistant to marry her in order to keep her visa status in the U.S. and avoid deportation to Canada

MacGregor and Barnes explain how the two characters in the movie transform their attitudes toward each other, all for the better in the end. We are always choosing. As described under Lens #4, it is always a choice to move up or down a level. The movie clearly shows how, in any situation, we can either change our attitude or change our situation.

Another final resource is *The Spiritual Cinema Circle*, which you can learn more about at ✦ www.spiritualcinemacircle.com. They provide a monthly subscription service where you can receive a set of DVD shorts and a feature length film. All films are meant to inspire with stories of courage, love, and transformation. Many stories are about raw coping power.

# End Notes

THIS SECTION PROVIDES A BRIEF LIST of relevant sources. To download a comprehensive list, please visit our website at www.rawcopingpower.com.

## Introduction Notes

1. FOR MORE SELF EXPLORATION OF ARCHETYPES, see Myss, C. (2013). Archetypes: Who Are You? Carlsbad, CA: Hay House; visit www.myss.com/library/contracts; and Pearson, C. (1998). The Hero Within; Six Archetypes We Live By. New York: Harper Collins; visit www.herowithin.com

2. MANY DIFFERENT CONCEPTS proposed by psychologists speak to an in-born motivation to strive and actualize our destiny.

    Maslow, A.H. (1968). *Toward a Psychology of Being*. New York: Van Nostrand.

    Frankl, V.E. (1985). *Man's Search for Meaning*. New York: Washington Square Press

    Deci, E.L., & Ryan, R.M. (1985). *Self-Determination*. Hoboken, N.J.: John Wiley & Sons, Inc.

    Csikszentmihalyi, M. (2009). *Creativity: Flow and the Psychology of Discovery*. New York: Harper Collins.

    Bandura, A. (1994). *Self-efficacy*. Hoboken, N.J.: John Wiley & Sons, Inc.

    Maddi, S.R. (2006). Hardiness: The courage to grow from stresses. *The Journal of Positive Psychology*, 1(3), 160–168.

3. TWO SOURCE MATERIALS on the work of Hans Selye and Aaron Antonovsky:

> Selye, H. (1956). *The Stress of Life*. Republished in 1978. Oxford, England: McGraw-Hill.

> Antonovsky, A. (1987). *Unraveling the Mystery of Health: How People Manage Stress and Stay Well*. San Francisco: Jossey-Bass.

4. MANY OF THE IDEAS in *Raw Coping Power* are derived from two primary training programs: Team Awareness and Team Resilience. Information on these programs can be found in the National Registry of Evidence-Based Programs and Practices.

> For Team Awareness:
> www.nrepp.samhsa.gov/ViewIntervention.aspx?id=69
> For Team Resilience:
> www.nrepp.samhsa.gov/ViewIntervention.aspx?id=285

Here is a brief list of research articles that show evidence for effectiveness with a brief description of outcomes.

> Petree, R.D., Broome, K., & Bennett, J.B. (2012). Exploring and reducing stress in young restaurant workers: Results of a randomized field trial. *American Journal of Health Promotion*, 6(4), 217–224. KEY OUTCOMES: Reduced stress, evidence of social diffusion of stress management skills, improvement of work climate.

> Patterson, C.R., Bennett, J.B., & Wiitala, W.L. (2005). Healthy and unhealthy stress unwinding: Promoting health in small businesses. *Journal of Business and Psychology*, 20(2), 221–247. KEY OUTCOMES: Improved use of healthy coping skills.

> Bennett, J.B., Patterson, C.R., Reynolds, G.S., Wiitala, W.L., and Lehman, W.E.K. (2004). Team awareness, problem drinking, and drinking climate: Workplace social health promotion in a policy context. *American Journal of Health Promotion*, 19(2), 103–113. KEY OUTCOMES: Improved work climate, reduced stigma for seeking health, reductions in problem drinking, improved productivity.

5. YOUR INNER GUARDIAN. For readers interested in learning more, some suggested works are given here:

> Deikman, A.J. (1983). *The Observing Self: Mysticism and Psychotherapy*. Boston: Beacon Press.

Hayes, S.C., & Smith, S. (2005). *Get Out of Your Mind and Into Your Life: The New Acceptance and Commitment Therapy*. Oakland, Calif.: New Harbinger Publications.

Almaas, A.H. (1986). *Essence: The Diamond Approach to Inner Realization*. Newburyport, Mass.: Red Wheel Weiser.

Watts, A. (2000). *Still the Mind: An Introduction to Meditation*. Novato, Calif.: New World Library.

Wilber, K. (1998). *The Eye of Spirit*. Boston: Shambhala Publications.

6. THE RESEARCH IS CLEAR that context matters:

Sommers, S. (2011). *Situations Matter: Understanding How Context Transforms Your World*. Westminster, London: Penguin Group.

Nolan, J.M., Schultz, P.W., Cialdini, R.B., Goldstein, N.J., & Griskevicius, V. (2008). Normative social influence is underdetected. *Personality and Social Psychology Bulletin, 34*(7), 913–923.

Bohns, V.K., & Flynn, F. J. (2013). Underestimating our influence over others at work. *Research in Organizational Behavior, 33*, 97–112.

7. JOB STRESS. In one of our studies using tools similar to those here, we found that workers chose more positive ways to unwind. This study was Patterson, C.R., Bennett, J.B., & Wiitala, W.L., (2005). Healthy and unhealthy stress unwinding: Promoting health in small businesses. *Journal of Business and Psychology, 20*(2), 221–247.

8. OUR WORK WITH THE MILITARY involved a seven-year consultation with the National Guard, where we translated and adapted the Team Awareness material into a program known as Team Readiness. More information about Team Readiness can be obtained by contacting the author.

9. YOUR BOSS: One of our programs trains managers in a more compassionate approach. The online e-learning program ExecuPrev™ is based on the LeadWell, LiveWell approach. This is discussed in my book *Heart-Centered Leadership* coauthored with Susan Steinbrecher. Results from a randomized clinical trial showed reductions in stress among managers receiving the ExecuPrev™ program. See Bennett, J.B., Broome, K., Gilmore, P., & Pilley, A. (2011). A web-based approach to address cardiovascular risks

in managers: Results of a randomized trial. *Journal of Occupational & Environmental Medicine, 53*(8), 911–918.

## Chapter 1 Notes

1. FOR PRINCIPLE #2, WE MENTIONED that studies on the most effective ways to reduce job-related stress suggest that it is important to make improvements in the shared work environment.

> LaMontagne, A.D., Keegel, T., Louie, A.M., Ostry, A., & Landsbergis, P.A. (2007). A systematic review of the job-stress intervention evaluation literature, 1990–2005. *International Journal of Occupational and Environmental Health, 13*(3), 268–280.

> Goldgruber, J., & Ahrens, D. (2010). Effectiveness of workplace health promotion and primary prevention interventions: A review. *Journal of Public Health, 18*(1), 75–88.

> Bhui, K.S., Dinos, S., Stansfeld, S.A., & White, P.D. (2012). A synthesis of the evidence for managing stress at work: A review of the reviews reporting on anxiety, depression, and absenteeism. *Journal of Environmental and Public Health, 2012*, 1–21.

> David, A.R., & Szamoskozi, S. (2011). A meta-analytical study on the effects of cognitive behavioral techniques for reducing distress in organizations. *Journal of Cognitive & Behavioral Psychotherapies, 11*(2), 221–236.

2. FOR PRINCIPLE #3, WE MENTIONED that in addition to stress training, there are many easy-to-implement and effective activity programs available such as Booster Breaks, Instant Recess, or onsite stretching programs.

> Yance, T., & Yancey, A.K. (2010). *Instant Recess: Building a Fit Nation 10 Minutes at a Time.* Los Angeles: University of California Press.

> Taylor, W.C. (2005). Transforming work breaks to promote health. *American Journal of Preventive Medicine, 29*(5), 461–465.

> Largo-Wight, E., Chen, W.W., Dodd, V., & Weiler, R. (2011). Healthy workplaces: The effects of nature contact at work on employee stress and health. *Public Health Reports, 126* (Suppl. 1), 124–130.

3. PRINCIPLE #4 EXPLAINS HOW each of us tends to have a set-point.

Headey, B. (2010). The set-point theory of well-being has serious flaws: On the eve of a scientific revolution? *Social Indicators Research, 97*(1), 7–21.

Diener, E. (2012). New findings and future directions for subjective well-being research. *American Psychologist, 67*(8), 590–597.

Luhmann, M., Hofmann, W., Eid, M., & Lucas, R.E. (2012). Subjective well-being and adaptation to life events: A meta-analysis. *Journal of Personality and Social Psychology, 102*(3), 592–615.

Fredrickson, B.L., & Losada, M.F. (2005). Positive affect and the complex dynamics of human flourishing. *American Psychologist, 60*(7), 678–686.

4. PRINCIPLE # 5 EXPLAINS THAT IF ONE individual in the group gets "too happy" or "too successful," there may be social pressure for that person to conform to a lower level of health or success.

Burke, R.J., & Cooper, C.L. (Eds.). (2013). *Voice and Whistleblowing in Organizations: Overcoming Fear, Fostering Courage and Unleashing Candour.* Cheltenham, UK: Edward Elgar Publishing.

Smith, E.R., Seger, C.R., & Mackie, D.M. (2007). Can emotions be truly group level? Evidence regarding four conceptual criteria. *Journal of Personality and Social Psychology, 93*(3), 431–446.

Christakis, N.A., & Fowler, J.H. (2009). *Connected: The Surprising Power of Our Social Networks and How They Shape Our Lives.* New York: Hachette Digital, Inc.

5. ADDICTIVE PROCESSES ARE A MAJOR factor in keeping us unaware of many of the processes discussed in this book. This lack of awareness is often labeled as "denial" in therapeutic literature. The prevalence of addictive processes cannot be underrated. Sussman and colleagues (2011) suggest that as much as 47 percent of the U.S. adult population suffers from maladaptive signs of an addictive disorder. Social norms, mostly operating at an unconscious level, also influence us.

Sussman, S., Lisha, N., & Griffiths, M. (2011). Prevalence of the addictions: A problem of the majority or the minority? *Evaluation & The Health Professions, 34*(1), 3–56.

Neighbors, C., Lee, C.M., Lewis, M.A., Fossos, N., & Larimer, M.E. (2007). Are social norms the best predictor of outcomes among heavy-drinking college students?. *Journal of Studies on Alcohol and Drugs, 68*(4), 556–565.

Schaef, A.W. (1988). *When Society Becomes an Addict.* San Francisco: HarperCollins.

Howard, M., McMillen, C., Nower, L., Elze, D., Edmond, T., & Bricout, J. (2002). Denial in addiction: Toward an integrated stage and process model—qualitative findings. *Journal of Psychoactive Drugs, 34*(4), 371–382.

Rinn, W., Desai, N., Rosenblatt, H., & Gastfriend, D.R. (2002). Addiction denial and cognitive dysfunction: A preliminary investigation. *The Journal of Neuropsychiatry and Clinical Neurosciences, 14*(1), 52–57.

6. ONE EXAMPLE OF AN ORGANIZATION that promotes awareness of problems is the National Health Service in Great Britain that posts and disseminates examples of individuals. As of January 2014 twelve well-documented cases have been posted at "A Better NHS" www.ajustnhs.com/ see specifically, www.ajustnhs.com/case-histories-of-victimised-nhs-staff/.

7. THE DEFINITIONS PROVIDED HERE—of adversity, resilience, and thriving, for example—are informed by several key resources.

O'Leary, V.E., & Ickovics, J.R. (1995). Resilience and thriving in response to challenge: An opportunity for a paradigm shift in women's health. *Women's Health, 1*(2), 121–142.

Carver, C.S. (1998). Resilience and thriving: Issues, models, and linkages. *Journal of Social Issues, 54*(2), 245–266.

Bonanno, G.A., & Mancini, A.D. (2008). The human capacity to thrive in the face of potential trauma. *Pediatrics, 121*(2), 369–375.

Maslow, A.H. (1959). Cognition of being in the peak experiences. *The Journal of Genetic Psychology, 94*(1), 43–66.

Rambo, L.R. (1993). *Understanding Religious Conversion.* New Haven, Conn.: Yale University Press.

Keyes, C.L. (2010). *Flourishing.* Hoboken, N.J.: John Wiley & Sons, Inc.

Ryff, C.D. (1989). Happiness is everything, or is it? Explorations on the meaning of psychological well-being. *Journal of Personality and Social Psychology, 57,* 1069–1081.

Fredrickson, B.L., & Losada, M.F. (2005). Positive affect and the complex dynamics of human flourishing. *American Psychologist, 60*(7), 678–686.

8. IN THE DISCUSSION OF PRINCIPLE #7, a study is described in which employees in organizations that had higher work stress were actually less

likely to contact their employee assistance programs (EAP). See Bennett, J., & Broome, K. (2010). Stress at and away from work: An ICAS Whitepaper. Available from the author. Contact: learn@organizationalwellness.com.

9. FOR MORE INFORMATION ON KRIS CARR and Cancer recovery, see

> Carr, K. (2008). *Crazy Sexy Cancer Survivor: More Rebellion and Fire for Your Healing Journey.* Guilford, Conn.: Globe Pequot.
>
> Langreth, R. (2009). Cancer miracles. *Forbes* (February). Accessed at www.forbes.com/forbes/2009/0302/074_cancer_miracles.html.
>
> Stage IV hope. A website dedicated to documenting, in as objective a way as possible, stories of recovery. Visit www.stage4hope.org.

## Chapter 3 Notes

1. LENS #1, THE STRESSOR-STRAIN MODEL, is the most widespread model of stress in the field of workplace stress studies.

> Andrews, G., Tennant, C., Hewson, D.M., & Vaillant, G.E. (1978). Life event stress, social support, coping style, and risk of psychological impairment. *The Journal of Nervous and Mental Disease*, 166(5), 307–316.
>
> Cohen, S., & Wills, T.A. (1985). Stress, social support, and the buffering hypothesis. *Psychological Bulletin*, 98(2), 310–357.
>
> Lazarus, R.S. (1966). *Psychological Stress and the Coping Process.* New York: McGraw-Hill.

THE NATIONAL INSTITUTE OF OCCUPATIONAL Safety & Health (NIOSH) uses this linear model in its 1999 public awareness booklet titled "Stress ... at Work" DHHS (NIOSH) Publication Number 99-101. This booklet can be accessed at www.cdc.gov/niosh/docs/99-101/ and downloaded at. www.cdc.gov/niosh/docs/99-101/pdfs/99-101.pdf.

2. LENS #1 DISCUSSES TRANSFORMATION, which has some of its roots in transpersonal psychology, a field of psychology devoted to studying higher levels of consciousness, spirituality, and transcendent aspects of human experience.

> Metzner, R. (1980). Ten classical metaphors of self-transformation. *Journal of Transpersonal Psychology*, 12(1), 47–62.

Schlitz, M.M., Vieten, C., & Amorok, T. (2008). *Living Deeply: The Art and Science of Transformation in Everyday Life*. Oakland, Calif.: New Harbinger Publications.

Wilber, K., Engler, J., & Brown, D. (1986). *Transformations of Consciousness: Conventional and Contemplative Perspectives on Development*. Boston: Shambhala.

3. Lens #1 explains how social support is perhaps the most well-established buffer of stress.

Uchino, B.N., Cacioppo, J.T., & Kiecolt-Glaser, J.K. (1996). The relationship between social support and physiological processes: A review with emphasis on underlying mechanisms and implications for health. *Psychological Bulletin, 119*(3), 488–531.

Holt-Lunstad, J., Smith, T.B., & Layton, J.B. (2010). Social relationships and mortality risk: A meta-analytic review. *PLoS Medicine, 7*(7), e1000316.

Kossek, E.E., Pichler, S., Bodner, T., & Hammer, L.B. (2011). Workplace social support and work-family conflict: A meta-analysis clarifying the influence of general and work-family, specific supervisor and organizational support. *Personnel Psychology, 64*(2), 289–313.

4. Here are some key articles on post-traumatic growth.

Zoellner, T., & Maercker, A. (2006). Post-traumatic growth in clinical psychology—A critical review and introduction of a two component model. *Clinical Psychology Review, 26*(5), 626–653.

Prati, G., & Pietrantoni, L. (2009). Optimism, social support, and coping strategies as factors contributing to post-traumatic growth: A meta-analysis. *Journal of Loss and Trauma, 14*(5), 364–388.

Lelorain, S., Bonnaud-Antignac, A., & Florin, A. (2010). Long-term post-traumatic growth after breast cancer: Prevalence, predictors and relationships with psychological health. *Journal of Clinical Psychology in Medical Settings, 17*(1), 14–22.

Linley, P.A., & Joseph, S. (2004). Positive change following trauma and adversity: A review. *Journal of Traumatic Stress, 17*(1), 11–21.

5. In Lens #2, we mention that there is actually research into the idea that "What doesn't kill us makes us stronger." Dr. Mark Seery (University of

Buffalo) examines factors that lead people to either be vulnerable or strong in the face of adversity. See a list of his publications at http://seery.socialpsychology.org/publications.

6. FOR THE STORY ON JOHN MACKEY AND WHOLE FOODS, see these references:

Collins, B. (2013). John Mackey, Whole Foods: Ethical appetite. *Billionaire* (May 29, 2013). Accessed at www.billionaire.com/wisdom/417/john-mackey-whole-foods-ethical-appetite.

CEO: John Mackey, Whole Foods Market (2013). Interview with Lee Cullum from KERA Television (broadcast, March 2013). Accessed at www.kera.org/2013/03/27/john-mackey-whole-foods-market.

Strong, M., & Mackey, J. (2009). *Be the Solution: How Entrepreneurs and Conscious Capitalists Can Solve All the World's Problems.* Hoboken, N.J.: Wiley.com.

Mackey, J., & Sisodia, R. (2013). *Conscious Capitalism.* Harvard Business Review Press, Boston.

7. NEUROPLASTICITY. The field of neuroplasticity as it relates to adversity and resilience is still quite new. These technical articles provide a diverse sampling for interested readers:

Karatsoreos, I.N., & McEwen, B.S. (2013). Resilience and vulnerability: A neurobiological perspective. *F1000prime reports, 5.* Accessed at www.ncbi.nlm.nih.gov/pmc/articles/PMC3643078/.

Cicchetti, D. (2010). Resilience under conditions of extreme stress: A multilevel perspective. *World Psychiatry, 9*(3), 145–154.

Radley, J.J., Kabbaj, M., Jacobson, L., Heydendael, W., Yehuda, R., & Herman, J.P. (2011). Stress risk factors and stress-related pathology: Neuroplasticity, epigenetics and endophenotypes. *Stress, 14*(5), 481–497.

8. CONNECTIVITY AT THE NEURAL LEVEL has a parallel at the experiential level in the form of compassion. See this article: Davidson, R.J., & McEwen, B.S. (2012). Social influences on neuroplasticity: Stress and interventions to promote well-being. *Nature Neuroscience, 15*(5), 689–695.

9. FOR IDEAS ABOUT RADICAL ACCEPTANCE, see Brach, T. (2003). *Radical Acceptance: Embracing Your Life with the Heart of a Buddha.* New York: Bantam.

10. THE IDEA OF POTENTIATION IS INFORMED by these key concepts, for which there are many studies. Only some initial references for each are provided.

For *self-efficacy*, see Bandura, A. (1977). Self-efficacy: Toward a unifying theory of behavioral change. *Psychological Review, 84*(2), 191–215.

For *psychological capital*, see Luthans, F., Youssef, C.M., & Avolio, B.J. (2006). *Psychological Capital: Developing the Human Competitive Edge*. Oxford, UK: Oxford University Press.

For *self-leadership*, see Stewart, G.L., Courtright, S.H., & Manz, C.C. (2011). Self-leadership: A multilevel review. *Journal of Management, 37*(1), 185–222.

For *self-determination*, see Ryan, R.M., & Deci, E.L. (2000). Self-determination theory and the facilitation of intrinsic motivation, social development, and well-being. *American Psychologist, 55*(1), 68–78.

For *hardiness*, see Eschleman, K.J., Bowling, N.A., & Alarcon, G.M. (2010). A meta-analytic examination of hardiness. *International Journal of Stress Management, 17*(4), 277–307.

For *flourishing and thriving*, see Keyes, C.L., & Haidt, J.E. (2003). *Flourishing: Positive Psychology and the Life Well-Lived*. Hoboken, N.J.: John Wiley & Sons, Inc.; and

Spreitzer, G., Sutcliffe, K., Dutton, J., Sonenshein, S., & Grant, A.M. (2005). A socially embedded model of thriving at work. *Organization Science, 16*(5), 537–549.

For *collective efficacy*, see Bandura A. (2000). Exercise of human agency through collective efficacy. *Current Directions in Psychological Science 9*(3), 75–78.

For *team resilience*, see Bennett, J.B., Aden, C.A., Broome, K., Mitchell, K., & Rigdon, W.D. (2010). Team resilience for young restaurant workers: Research-to-practice adaptation and assessment. *Journal of Occupational Health Psychology, 15*(3), 223–236.

11. LENS #4 REFERENCES A CLINICAL STUDY with Team Resilience, where we assessed employees' stress and productivity one year after they received some of the tools in this book. This study is Petree, R.D., Broome, K., Bennett, J.B. (2012). Exploring and reducing stress in young restaurant workers: Results of a randomized field trial. *American Journal of Health Promotion, 6*(4), 217–224.

12. For Lens # 5 on Centering, Community, Compassion, Confidence, and Commitment. The Five Cs of resilience were developed from a review of the resilience literature in 2005 and by comparing and contrasting different theories and measures available at that time. Key references for this model include the following:

Maddi, S.R. (2005). On hardiness and other pathways to resilience. *American Psychologist, 59*(1), 20–28.

Friborg, O., Barlaug, D., Martinussen, M., Rosenvinge, J.H., & Hjemdal, O. (2005). Resilience in relation to personality and intelligence. *International Journal of Methods in Psychiatric Research, 14*(1), 29–42.

Clausen, J. (1993). *American Lives: Looking Back at the Children of the Great Depression.* New York: Free Press.

Bonnano, G.A. (2004). Loss, trauma, and human resilience: Have we underestimated the human capacity to thrive after extremely aversive events? *American Psychologist, 59,* 20–28.

Rutter, M. (1985). Resilience in the face of adversity: Protective factors and resistance to psychiatric disorder. *British Journal of Psychiatry 147,* 598–611.

Werner, E., & R. Smith. (1989). *Vulnerable but Invincible: A Longitudinal Study of Resilient Children and Youth.* New York: Adams, Bannister, and Cox.

Ahern, N.R., Kiehl, E.M., Lou Sole, M., & Byers, J. (2006). A review of instruments measuring resilience. *Issues in Comprehensive Pediatric Nursing, 29*(2), 103–125.

13. Why does addiction happen? Different answers from science have been tested and different solutions have been shown to work. This is a difficult area to summarize because there are different types of addictions (such as tobacco, alcohol, drugs, sexual), different types of treatments for each (such as individual, group, 12-step, pharmaceutical), and different theories. The idea of negative coping cycle is only one of many explanations.

Bradshaw, J. (2005). *Healing the Shame that Binds You.* Deerfield Beach, Fla.: HCI.

Elster, J. (2000). *Strong Feelings: Emotion, Addiction, and Human Behavior.* Massachusetts Institute of Technology: MIT Press.

Dearing, R.L., Stuewig, J., & Tangney, J.P. (2005). On the importance of distinguishing shame from guilt: Relations to problematic alcohol and drug use. *Addictive Behaviors, 30*(7), 1392–1404.

Wiechelt, S.A. (2007). The specter of shame in substance misuse. *Substance Use & Misuse, 42*(2-3), 399–409.

Firman, J. (1997). *The Primal Wound: A Transpersonal View of Trauma, Addiction, and Growth.* New York: SUNY Press.

Garland, E.L., Fredrickson, B., Kring, A.M., Johnson, D.P., Meyer, P.S., & Penn, D.L. (2010). Upward spirals of positive emotions counter downward spirals of negativity: Insights from the broaden-and-build theory and affective neuroscience on the treatment of emotion dysfunctions and deficits in psychopathology. *Clinical Psychology Review, 30*(7), 849–864.

Wood, A.M., Froh, J.J., & Geraghty, A.W. (2010). Gratitude and well-being: A review and theoretical integration. *Clinical Psychology Review, 30*(7), 890–905.

14. THE DISCUSSION OF LENS #7, THE NEGATIVE COPING CYCLE, explains how society also plays a role in addiction by how it fosters, normalizes, advertises, and provides access to addictive substances. There is a substantial and complex literature on how culture can support and foster addictive tendencies.

Sussman, S., Lisha, N., & Griffiths, M. (2011). Prevalence of the addictions: A problem of the majority or the minority?. *Evaluation & The Health Professions, 34*(1), 3–56.

Schaef, A.W. (1988). *When Society Becomes an Addict.* San Francisco: HarperCollins.

White. W. (1996). *Pathways from the Culture of Addiction to the Culture of Recovery: A Travel Guide for Addiction Professionals.* Center City, Minn.: Hazelden.

15. TEAM AWARENESS. The concept of team awareness was originally discussed in Bennett and Lehman (2000) and Lehman, Reynolds, and Bennett (2003) with specific application to substance abuse prevention.

Bennett, J.B., Lehman, W.E.K., & Reynolds, G.S. (2000) Team awareness for workplace substance abuse prevention: The empirical and conceptual development of a training program. *Prevention Science, 1*(3), 157–172.

Lehman, W.E.K., Reynolds, G.S., & Bennett, J.B. (2003). Team and informational training for workplace substance abuse prevention. In J.B. Bennett & W.E.K. Lehman (Eds). *Workplace Substance Abuse Prevention: Beyond Drug Testing to Wellness.* Washington, D.C.: American Psychological Association.

16. MANAGER PATHWAYS FOR POTENTIATION. The five different pathways described were originally presented in Quick, J.C., Bennett, J.B., & Hargrove, M.B. (2014). Stress, health and wellbeing in practice: Workplace leadership and leveraging stress for positive outcome. In P. Chen & C.L. Cooper (Eds.), *Wellbeing in the Workplace: From Stress to Happiness.* Oxford and New York: Wiley-Blackwell.

17. THE *WE* IN WELLNESS. The eight different paths of the *We* in Wellness were originally described in Bennett, J.B. & Tetrick, L. (2013). The we in wellness: Workplace health promotion as a positive force for health in society. In J.B. Olson-Buchanan, L.L.K. Bryan, & L.F. Thompson (Eds.). *Using Industrial Organizational Psychology for the Greater Good: Helping Those Who Help Others.* London: Routledge.

18. RESEARCH ON MARITAL AND FAMILY strengthening programs shows that the application of these basic principles can work to help reduce stress and its negative impact. A good self-help resource is Gottman, J., Gottman, J.S., & DeClaire, J. (2007). *Ten Lessons to Transform Your Marriage: America's Love Lab Experts Share Their Strategies for Strengthening Your Relationship.* New York: Random House Digital, Inc.

19. SPECIFIC SKILLS CAN BE TAUGHT to family members who are dealing with the stress of having addiction in the family system. These are available through such tools as a 12-step program (Al-Anon) or a method called CRAFT (Community Reinforcement Approach and Family Training) by Robert J. Meyers, Ph.D. See Meyers, R.J., & Wolfe, B.L. (2009). Get your loved one sober: Alternatives to nagging, pleading, and threatening. Center City, Minn.: Hazelden.

## Chapter 4 Notes

1. Here is background on stories at the beginning of this chapter. Chris Gardner is the man whose childhood was marked by poverty, domestic violence, alcoholism, sexual abuse, and family illiteracy. His story was told in the movie *The Pursuit of Happyness* (2006) starring Will Smith. You can read more about Chris through these links and interviews:

   His own website: www.chrisgardnermedia.com/

   Chiofolo, V. (2010, September 29). The Survivor: Catching up with Chris Gardner in *Trader Daily*. Accessed at www.traderdaily.com/09/the-survivor-chris-gardner/.

   Murray, R. (2006). Chris Gardner Talks about "The Pursuit of Happyness." Accessed at About.com (Hollywood Movies), and http://movies.about.com/od/thepursuitofhappyness/a/pursuitcg 120806.htm.

Ed Dobson has survived despite being told he only had two to five years left to live. You can learn more about his story at http://edsstory.com/.

2. Elaborate cognitive learning skills are a key part of building resilience.

   Weinstein, C.E., & Hume, L.M. (1998). *Study Strategies for Lifelong Learning*. Washington, D.C.: American Psychological Association.

   Weinstein, C.E. (1982). Training students to use elaboration learning strategies. *Contemporary Educational Psychology*, 7(4), 301–311.

   Bembenutty, H. (Ed.). (2011). *Self-Regulated Learning: New Directions for Teaching and Learning, Number 126*. San Francisco, Calif.: Jossey-Bass

3. The self-help references on communication skills include these:

   Kuhnke, E. (2013) *Communication Skills for Dummies*. England: John Wiley.

   Rosenberg, M.B. (2003). *Nonviolent Communication: A Language of Life: Create Your Life, Your Relationships, and Your World in Harmony with Your Values*. Encinitas, Calif.: PuddleDancer Press.

4. Some self-help resources on emotional intelligence:

   Stein, S.J. (2009). *Emotional Intelligence for Dummies*. Hoboken, N.J.: Wiley Publishing.

Goleman, D. (2006). *Emotional Intelligence: Why It Can Matter More Than IQ*. New York: Bantam Books.

Segal, J. (2008). *The Language of Emotional Intelligence: The Five Essential Tools for Building Powerful and Effective Relationships*. New York: McGraw-Hill.

5. FOR TOOL #19 ON GOAL-SETTING, the most effective form for an intention is the if/then format.

Gollwitzer, P.M. (1999). Implementation intentions: Strong effects of simple plans. *American Psychologist, 54*(7), 493–503.

Gollwitzer, P.M., & Sheeran, P. (2006). Implementation intentions and goal achievement: A meta-analysis of effects and processes. *Advances in Experimental Social Psychology, 38,* 69–119.

6. FOR TOOLS #22 AND #23 THERE is substantial research on uplifts and positive experiences. See these examples:

Kanner, A.D., Coyne, J.C., Schaefer, C., & Lazarus, R.S. (1981). Comparison of two modes of stress measurement: Daily hassles and uplifts versus major life events. *Journal of Behavioral Medicine, 4*(1), 1–39.

Tugade, M.M., & Fredrickson, B.L. (2004). Resilient individuals use positive emotions to bounce back from negative emotional experiences. *Journal of Personality and Social Psychology, 86*(2), 320–333.

Frerickson, B. (2009). *Positivity: Top-notch Research Reveals the 3 to 1 Ratio That Will Change Your Life*. New York: Three Rivers Press.

7. FOR TOOL #24 ON VISUALIZATION, there is a growing body of research on hope and optimism within the broad field of positive psychology and at work. A recent systematic review by Bolier and colleagues (2013) suggests that interventions designed to enhance hope and optimism can be effective. Reichard and colleagues (2013) also found a positive relationship between hope and work performance.

Bolier, l., Haverman, M., Hesterhof, G.J., Riper, H., Smit, F., & Bohlmeijer, E. (2013). Positive psychology interventions: a meta-analysis of randomized controlled studies. *BMC Public Health, 13*(1), 119–139.

Reichard, R.J., Avey, J.B., Lopez, S., & Dollwet, M. (2013). Having the will and finding the way: a review and meta-analysis of hope at work. *The Journal of Positive Psychology, 8*(4), 1–13.

8. FOR TOOL #25 ON JOB CRAFTING, there is a new and growing area of research. Here are some additional references and resources.

Wrzesniewski, A., & Dutton, J.E. (2001). Crafting a job: Revisioning employees as active crafters of their work. *Academy of Management Review, 26*(2), 179–201.

Tims, M., Bakker, A.B., & Derks, D. (2012). Development and validation of the job crafting scale. *Journal of Vocational Behavior, 80*(1), 173–186.

Petrou, P., Demerouti, E., Peeters, M.C., Schaufeli, W.B., & Hetland, J. (2012). Crafting a job on a daily basis: Contextual correlates and the link to work engagement. *Journal of Organizational Behavior, 33*(8), 1120–1141.

Kirkendall, Cristina D. (2013). *Job Crafting: The Pursuit of Happiness at Work.* Diss. Wright State University.

9. TOOL #27, THRIVE MAPPING, is an example of cognitive mapping.

Hall, R.H., & O'Donnell, A. (1996). Cognitive and affective outcomes of learning from knowledge maps. *Contemporary Educational Psychology, 21*(1), 94–101.

O'Donnell, A.M., Dansereau, D.F., & Hall, R.H. (2002). Knowledge maps as scaffolds for cognitive processing. *Educational Psychology Review, 14*(1), 71–86.

10. ON TOOL #28, WORK-LIFE BORDERS:

Clark, S.C. (2000). Work/family border theory: A new theory of work/family balance. *Human Relations, 53*(6), 747–770.

# Acknowledgments

My first and primary thanks go to my wife and companion, Jan, for providing valuable feedback on drafts and many supportive and insightful conversations over our twenty years of thriving from life's challenges together.

The material for this book comes from three streams of support that have helped shape my thinking. First are the teachers and education stations along my personal resilience journey. Without support and guidance coming from this stream, I would never have had the direct experience that stress could be a teacher and friend.

These teachers include my parents (Jerry Bennett and Jane Shapiro Bennett), my brother (Steven), Robert Neville, Richard J. Davidson, Oscar Ichazo, Janet Spence, Anne Wilson Schaef, Chloe Wordsworth, Jack Kornfeld, Joseph Goldstein, Sharon Salzberg, Sue-Anne MacGregor, Dorinda Hartson, Gary Berman, and Farrel Brenner; and also my friends and colleagues in key groups that showed me how to access my own raw coping power: Arica, The Insight Meditation Society, Al-Anon, Living in Process, The Society of Friends (Quakers), Resonance Repatterning, and Radha Soami Satsang Beas. Thanks also to others who really showed up to help me get in touch with my own resilience during difficult times: Joey Walker, Walt Ayotte, Jeff Berman, Vincent Guardia.

Second, the practical foundation and original research comes from studies conducted when I was employed as a scientist at the Institute of Behavioral Research (IBR) at Texas Christian University, where my work was supported by Wayne Lehman and Dwayne Simpson and in collaboration with my colleagues Norma Bartholomew, Shawn Reynolds, and Kirk Broome.

Beginning in 1994, my work at the IBR led to the original Stress Management module from the Team Awareness curriculum, and this module formed the initial basis for the Raw Coping Power training program. Stemming from this work and over the past two decades, many colleagues and clients have expressed confidence in me and our wise programs at my company, Organizational Wellness & Learning Systems (OWLS). Through their confidence, I was able to find a renewed energy to write this book.

These include Royer Cook, Deborah Galvin, Peggy Quigg, Johnny Boatman and the National Guard Prevention Coordinators, Denise Harvey (Ripley), Michaela Conley, Rohit Kantor, Sue-Anne MacGregor, Gary Cole, Ladonna Coy, Roger Jahnke, Bill Baun, Mark Attridge, Leonard Bade, Susan Steinbrecher, Jim Quick, Spencer Seidman, Richard Sledz, Connie Tyne, Gary Loper and Chris O'Neill.

Special mention needs to be made of key staff at OWLS who have helped in some way over the years to help me strengthen and sharpen the message of *Raw Coping Power* through over ten years of studies that we carried out together. These include Ashleigh Schwab, Charles (Chuck) A. Aden, Dave Rigdon, Kirk Broome (again), Renee Schuh, Heather Cline, Sherzine McKenzie, Kathryn Mitchell, Michelle Zadrozny, Ruth Ayn Ferguson, Janie Williams, Michael Neeper, Robyn Petree, Marsha Rainwater, and Karline Chapman. And to many others who have helped OWLS to thrive along the way, including Aaron, Magda, Emily, Lauren, Jodi, Pam, Logan, Trevor, Jessica, and Ken. I kept saying I could not do it without you guys and hopefully now you have some proof.

Throughout this book, I talk about social support and a special shout out to family and friends for warmth, laughter, and fun! Thanks to Daddy; James and Brittney; Matt and Tamara and Tyler; Danielle, Areanna, and Brooke; Tenzin; Morgan; Mike and Melissa; Channing and Robert; and the entire extended Murphy clan.

Also, gratitude for feedback from readers of drafts (Dave Sharar, Wendy Hovey, Renee Schuh, Duane Piety) and my wonderful editors Sandra Wendel, Nancy Bartosek Strini, and Julia Vaughan. You too, Ken Hogan for the lens and principles images. Appreciation to TheBookDesigner.com and Tracy Atkins and Joel Friedlander for their guidance on printing.

Finally, a special thanks to Mark Grant (MA, Clinical Psychologist) whose self-help relaxation tape "Calm and Confident" provided inspiration for the title of this book.

# About the Author

Joel B. Bennett, PhD, is President of Organizational Wellness & Learning Systems (OWLS), an international consulting firm that specializes in evidence-based wellness and e-learning technologies to promote organizational health, employee well-being, and stress transformation.

Dr. Bennett first delivered stress management programming in 1985. Since then, OWLS programs have reached over 30,000 employees across the United States. He is primary developer of Team Awareness and Team Resilience, two evidence-based programs recognized by the U.S. Department of Health and Human Services as effective in reducing employee behavioral risks. Team Awareness has been adapted by the U.S. National Guard as one of their flagship prevention programs. The training protocol has been used by restaurants, electrician training centers, small businesses, Native American tribal government, and in South Africa.

OWLS clients include corporate, private, nonprofit, local and federal agencies. OWLS has received close to $4 million in Federal Research Grants to assess, design, and deliver behavioral health promotion and workplace wellness programs.

The company's service line includes the Small Business Wellness Initiative, IntelliPrev™, PrevTools™, ExecuPrev™ (leadwell, livewell), and TeamUpNow™.

Dr. Bennett is the principal investigator on landmark studies and author of over twenty peer-reviewed research articles reporting on those findings. He has authored/coauthored three books:

- *Heart-Centered Leadership: LeadWell, LiveWell*
- *Time & Intimacy: A New Science of Personal Relationships*
- *Preventing Workplace Substance Abuse: Beyond Drug Testing to Wellness.*

In 2008, he was acknowledged with the Service Leadership award from the National Wellness Institute. He earned his bachelor's degree in psychology and philosophy from State University of New York (Purchase) and his MA and PhD in psychology from the University of Texas-Austin.

To learn more about OWLS, visit www.organizationalwellness.com.

Dr. Bennett lives in Fort Worth and Austin, Texas, with his wife, Jan.

Made in the USA
Middletown, DE
20 April 2019